Dell's story is an example of the restoration Jesus offers to each of us. No wound is too deep and no experience too tragic for the Lord to scoop us up and offer sweet resolve. A beautiful example of God's faithfulness and relentless pursuit of us.

Dr. Nicole Johnson, Miss America 1999

This book will be a special blessing to anyone who has ever felt the anguish of a broken relationship caused by the cruelty or selfishness of someone you have trusted with your life! It will inspire you to recognize that God is still on the throne as Dell has bared her soul to tell you her incredible journey.

From the first time Dell and her husband entered the doors of our Church, it seemed that Dell was destined to experience the many miraculous events that happened there. These miracles not only happened to her, but they also bolstered her faith in spite of the anguish she suffered from failed relationships. Sharon and I have considered Delbert as one of our daughters, and we have watched with pride as God put her and Cary together for an unusually beautiful loving relationship! Unchained is mesmerizing! You won't be able to put it down.

Dr. Marty Tharp PhD
Pastor/Evangelist to the British Isles
Singer/Musician
Author of 57 Books

It has been a long time since I've been this excited about the potential that Unchained has for deeply touching lives. Dell masterfully brings us into her world of tremendous pain and the Lord's passion to radically change lives that have been shattered. The devil almost won, but God had other plans as always. Sit back for a ride that will build your faith to believe God for the supernatural in every aspect of your life.

Wayne Dery
Founder and President of The Plant International

Dell Anderson has written a breathtakingly honest, page-turning, account of a life that has miraculously survived. I'm reminded of words written by Gloria Gaither, "All I had to offer Him was brokenness and strife, but He made something beautiful of my life." UNCHAINED offers living proof of our great God who can and will, indeed, make all things brand new.

Arthelene Rippy,
Producer / Host of Homekeepers
CHRISTIAN TELEVISION NETWORK

Thanks to my friend, Dell Anderson, for her masterful ability and willingness to tell her story. I remember her praying to receive healing from her memories. God answered. Now, she has prayed to remember so that her healing will help others going through painful moments. This is a compelling book that is just about impossible to put down until you finish it.

Tom Benigas
Missionary to Europe
Continental Theological Seminary/
European International Churches

Dell Anderson, through her courage and authenticity in her personal story, has provided a tool to help heal your past through her book. As you read "Unchained," you will find emotions of your own pain from the past being stirred yet given the solution through the overwhelming love of Jesus and the power of forgiveness.

The most critical piece for a healthy soul is our ability to heal our wounds from our past. Dell's life experience and history with God set a great example of what to do and what not to do with our pain…"It was impossible for me to heal from a wound I denied receiving." ~ Dell Anderson. The life lessons that can be learned from this book are invaluable. Thank you, Dell, for your bravery to be transparent and your perseverance to allow your story to become a place of Hope.

Matt Pfaltzgraf
Senior Pastor
One Life Community Church
Newman, Georgia
Founder and Director of The Green House Affect Project

In the years that I worked as a producer for *the 700 Club* I heard few testimonies as powerful as Dell Andersons. Her story of abuse and forgiveness, pain and healing blessed thousands when it first aired on the program and more than 500 people received Jesus Christ as their savior that day. Now, with this book, readers can hear the whole story that was impossible to tell in just a few short minutes on television. Read this book and your faith will grow as you learn of the healing, redemption and miracles Dell experienced. Don't miss this opportunity to hear a message of hope and restoration for anyone who has been broken and wounded, needing the healing touch of our Savior.

Linda Vulcano
Former reporter/producer The 700 Club

UNCHAINED

FROM THE SHACKLES OF THE PAST
TO A LIFE OF FREEDOM AND JOY

DELL ANDERSON

Dellanderson.unchained@gmail.com

Scriptures taken from the Holy Bible,

New International Version®, NIV®.
Copyright © 1973, 1978, 1984, 2011 by Biblica, Inc.
™ Used by permission of Zondervan.

All rights reserved worldwide. www.zondervan.com
The "NIV" and "New International Version" are trademarks
registered in the United States Patent and Trademark Office by
Biblica, Inc.™

All rights reserved. No part of this book may be reproduced
without written permission from the author. For information,
contact Dell Anderson at Dellanderson.unchained@gmail.com.

Edited by Phyllis Benigas

Cover illustration, layout and design: Laura (Musclow) Sebold

Printed in the United States of America 2018

Some names and identifying details have been changed to protect
the privacy of individuals.

In Loving Memory of
my mom and dad who sadly became
"UNCHAINED" only in their death.

CONTENTS

ACKNOWLEDGMENTS

I wish to express my sincere, heartfelt gratitude:

To Phyllis Benigas, my friend who birthed the idea of this book over thirty years ago. She and her husband, Tom, live in Brussels, Belgium, and serve as missionaries to Europe. Phyllis graciously accepted the difficult task of being my editor in spite of her very busy schedule. Her godly wisdom and knowledge have guided me through every painful process of writing this book. She has been an encouragement through every phase of this assignment from God. Thank you, Phyllis. Ta-Dah – it's a wrap!

To Laura Sebold, who designed the cover and illustrated my visions. She handled the technical end of the process from laying out the book to getting it ready for print. Her talent is extraordinary. She added beauty to the printed page and made it look enticing and inviting, and she captured the essence of my story with her art. Laura has a God-given talent that is undeniable. We have been friends for many years. I'm so happy God put us together for this project.

To Pastor Matt and Judy Pfaltzgraf – from the time we were a host family when you ministered in our church until the present, we were destined to become family. As we opened our home, we were blessed with the favor of God by your approach to God's Word. You led us through SOZO ministry and were instrumental in helping recognize the lies of the enemy, replacing them with God's truth. God sent you into my life to encourage me through the difficult days of reliving my past. Your lives exemplify kingdom living as you minister with boldness and truth. Thank you, Matt and Judy. You have been instrumental in my quest for inner healing.

To Pastor Ken and Laura Hope – You have been so encouraging through this journey. I learned so much during your facilitation of the BOAST School of Supernatural Ministry. To understand who I am in Christ has been instrumental during my healing process. My walk with my Father became so much closer as I soaked in His presence. I took my place of royalty as a child of the King. As a princess, I was able to go boldly to the throne. I communed with God on a deeper level as He wrapped me in His loving embrace. Thank you for your love and faithfulness to the work of the Lord.

To my family and friends – A great big thank you for all your love and encouragement, especially my beautiful daughters, Ashley and Courtney. Your prayers and kind words have cheered me on as I tackled the most difficult assignment of my life. There were times I wanted to quit, but you encouraged me to continue even in my pain. Thank you for believing in me. I love you to the moon and back.

To my firstborn son, Cliff – Because of you, I am alive to share my story. You were a bright light in the darkest time of my life. Because I tried to save you in that horrible car accident, my life was spared. When I was on my way to Heaven, I turned around at the sound of your cries begging me to come back to you. I love you now and always.

To my son, D.J. – You have brought new joy into our lives. You have been a blessing, and we love you with all our hearts. We are so happy that you came into our lives, and we can call you son.

To Wayne Dery – Your prayer for me to become unchained from the memories and pain of the past became the inspiration for the title of my book. At the moment you prayed, I physically heard the chains clang and fall to the floor.

My first born son, Cliff 2017

Ashley, Steve and Lonnie

Courtney, Darrell and
Carson 2015

My son, DJ, the fisherman

Family photo at Ashley's wedding. 2015. Happy Day.

My gramdsons,Carson and Lonnie

My granddaughter, Selena

FOREWORD

Once in a great while, we meet someone along the way and know immediately that our friendship will last forever. That's how it was the day I met Dell Anderson more than 30 years ago. Although we live a continent apart today, our friendship remains.

When Dell first shared her story with me over three decades ago, I knew that the world needed to hear it! Everyone needed to hear about the faithfulness of God throughout her incredible journey. We talked and dreamed about Dell writing a book about her life, and I offered any help I could give.

Have you noticed how life and all its details seem to usurp some of our goals and dreams? We both had young children, jobs and a myriad of responsibilities that consumed our time and those dreams were put on hold.

Over the next several years, I observed something unique about my friend. Dell was a magnet for lost and hurting people. Whether a co-worker, a neighbor or a store clerk, Dell attracted those facing challenging circumstances and in need of the Savior. She always had a testimony to share with me of how God used her story to bring someone to Him. Some things are meant to be.

In those early years, Dells story was compelling, and many lives were changed, but I like to say that it wasn't completely ripe. Now it is!

As you read Unchained, you will be captivated by her story and by the way she tells it. Be prepared to laugh a little and cry some. But even more significant, you will be challenged to trust the heart of God more than you ever have before.

Thank you, Dell, for sharing with the world your victory from the shackles of the past to freedom and joy.

Phyllis Benigas
Missionary to Europe
Continental Theological Seminary/
European International Churches

DEDICATION

With a joyful heart, I dedicate this book to my beloved husband, Cary. Cary has been a devoted husband and father for forty-one years. He fought for me in the trenches on his knees during my most difficult battles with the enemy. He has been my biggest cheerleader in times of success and my greatest advocate in the difficult times. His gentle nature and positive attitude have always encouraged me through the dark times. Cary has shown me the real meaning of a loving husband. His Godly character has been the moral compass for our children to follow. He is a true gift from God that I will cherish forever. Cary Anderson, I am so happy you chose me. Thank you for loving me.

Dr. Marty and Sharon Tharp – for leading me to Christ by not only teaching me about God's unconditional love but also showing me His love when I was broken and unlovable. You invited my son and me into your home and treated us like your own family until I could get on my feet. You gave me food, shelter and money at one of my lowest points. Under your ministry, I learned about God in a tangible way as I saw Him perform miracle after miracle on my behalf. I learned from Marty what a true shepherd is as he leads, sacrifices and cares for his flock. You will always be my spiritual mom and dad. I will always love you, Marty. I'm so glad you didn't pinch my head off when you threatened me so many times out of frustration.

Sandy Overstreet – my sister from another mother. No one could have a better friend than you. From our teen years until the present, you have saved me more times than I can count. You are the only person who has been with me through every heartache and every joyful celebration. Our friendship has stood the test of time and space. It is only fitting that you are the person who typed my manuscript. I'm not sure what would have happened to me without your friendship. I am grateful God knitted us together so long ago. No one can make me laugh like you do, Sandman. I love you, Sis.

To the Stranger – you didn't know me, and yet you opened your door to a woman who was naked and afraid. You gave me a hiding place and ultimately saved my life. You clothed me and told me how much Jesus loved me. Although in my desperation, I rejected your plea, you planted the seed that would later lead to my salvation. I don't know your name, but I know we will meet again someday in Heaven. You saved my life that night, and because you showed true agape love to a stranger, thousands have been saved and set free for the glory of God. Until we meet again, I remain eternally grateful.

INTRODUCTION

"Truly, I tell you there has never been a woman more blessed by God than me." These were the opening lines of a part I played in a performance entitled, "We Serve a Mighty God." Little did I realize that this statement would so perfectly describe my own story. As I began to meditate on these words, the reality of the awesomeness of God and how blessed I am consumed my every thought. God had given me all I could have hoped for and more. I have experienced the love of a devoted husband, four wonderful children, three grandchildren, a successful career and the sweetness of God's presence in my life. Although on the outside, my life with my husband, Cary, may appear to be a charmed life, the pain and turmoil of my past at one time threatened our marriage, my family, my health and my walk with God.

Many years ago, I felt a gentle nudge to tell my story, but it was not God's perfect timing. I tried to write this book more than thirty years ago, but I had to put it down because recalling those memories put me into a deep depression. I knew someday I would finish it. What I didn't know was the series of events that would catapult me into writing again. The Lord's leading has been so strong that I can no longer ignore His call on my life to minister to others who are hurting from the memories of their past. I have asked God over and over again, "Why have I been so hurt and riddled with pain throughout my life?" The answer I keep receiving is, "For such a time is this, for such a time is this."

I've come to realize that there are many people in the world, Christian and non-Christian alike, who suffer from the pain and guilt of their past. We are all victims of our past in one sense or another. It is as if we're walking through life with baggage in each hand. On one bag is a plus sign, and it contains all the positive experiences we have throughout life – love, success, achievements and all the strokes we receive that make us feel worthwhile. On the other bag is emblazoned a negative sign. As you've probably guessed, it's filled with all the negative experiences such as disappointments, hurts and failures. These painful memories are as varied as the many people who possess them, as none of us are fortunate enough to escape negativity in our life at one time or another. But, indeed, if our positive bag is not full to overflowing and the weight of the negative bag is not greatly overpowered by the positive experiences in our lives, we risk walking through life unbalanced.

It is to these people I wish to speak for there is emotional healing waiting to take place in their lives. As my story unfolds, there will be some of you who can relate to the pain and emotional trauma that I have experienced. If you are one of these people, I introduce you to the great Healer, Jesus Christ. Psalms 147:3 declares, "He heals the brokenhearted and binds up their wounds."

UNCHAINED

FROM THE SHACKLES OF THE PAST
TO A LIFE OF FREEDOM AND JOY

Chapter 1

You Will Live and Not Die

"You will live and not die." These six words continue to permeate through my being even today. It was December 6, 2014. The week started out like most weeks, full of the ups and downs of dealing with everyday struggles. Christmas was rapidly approaching, and I was overwhelmed with the busyness that accompanies the holidays. With all the shopping, gift-wrapping, decorating, party planning and events to attend, it was no wonder I felt tired and a bit stressed out.

I hadn't slept well all week from a persistent stabbing pain in my shoulder and neck. Thinking the pain was due to simple muscle spasms or a misalignment in my neck and spine, I went for chiropractic treatment. A good adjustment usually eased the pain, but this time the sharp pain continued with a vengeance.

Friday morning, after having very little sleep and feeling very despondent, I headed to church. Bethel Music from Redding, California was holding a three-day miracles conference, and I was eager to attend. As I entered the church, Pastor Ken Hope, the Executive Pastor of our church, greeted me. Service had already started as we headed for the front row to be seated.

As the band played and the people entered into worship, I tried to sing but was distracted by the stabbing pain in my shoulder. I looked out the corner of my eye, and in my peripheral vision, I saw a woman walk by in front of us. I didn't know her, but she had come with a group from another church that was hosting the event. She walked past me but then turned toward me. Our eyes met as she walked up to me and threw her arms around me in a loving embrace. As she held me, she began to speak into my ear. She spoke with authority and said these words which I will never forget. "You will live and not die." I pulled away, confused by her words, and then once again she said with piercing eyes, "The Lord says you will live and not die." Again I pulled away and wondered why she had approached me and spoken such profound words.

I didn't feel my best that day, but I certainly felt no impending doom. My heart was pounding, and one more time she spoke these words, "Do not fear, for the Lord says you will live and not die." She continued, "It's not your fault. The Lord says you are His princess, and He loves you with an everlasting love." I wondered what was happening! Then she continued, "The Lord says it is time." Two more times she repeated, "It is time." Immediately I thought, time for what?

Then she dropped the bomb that would prove to me that, indeed, she was hearing from God. She said, "It is time for you to write your book. The book you started so many years ago and couldn't finish because of your pain. The Lord is going to heal you of those memories so that many others will read your story and be healed for the glory of God. So write! God, Himself will give you the words." Then she pulled me close, smiled and whispered in my ear, "and I want the first copy." She turned and walked away and left me baffled by what had happened.

Pastor Ken heard the entire exchange, and he too was puzzled by her words. I knew without a doubt that I had received a word from God because she had no way of knowing that thirty years ago I started to write my story in book form but had to stop because it was too emotionally painful to relive my past.

I stayed until the end of the service and hurriedly headed home to tell my family about my experience. "You will live and not die" kept echoing in my mind. For two more sleepless nights, I lay in my bed rehearsing the event and pondering its meaning.

All day Monday I felt exhausted and rested much of the day. By the afternoon, I became short of breath and experienced a light pressure in the middle of my chest. Since I was no stranger to panic attacks, I dismissed my symptoms as just another episode of anxiety. I knew from experience that if I was quiet and still, symptoms would soon subside. When the feelings intensified, I decided to go to the after-hours clinic to be checked out.

My husband, Cary, drove me to the clinic. The clinic personnel took one look at me and began to scurry. After a blood test and EKG, they rushed me to the Hospital Emergency Room down the street. Tests were indicating that I was having a heart attack, and to say the least, the hours that followed were frightening. Cary called our children and best friends to inform them of my condition. I was admitted to the cardiac ward, and the cardiologist came in to speak to us. He said I needed a heart catheterization to determine the next course of action. I was in total disbelief, but now the prophetic words I had heard three days earlier became a reality and permeated my soul.

I was prepped for my procedure and rolled down to the cath lab. My husband and two daughters, Courtney and Ashley, followed waving and offering encouragement as I was rolled away. The fear in their eyes was obvious, and it shook me to my core.

When I awoke in my room, I was disoriented and felt like I had been hit by a truck. The cardiologist came in to deliver the devastating report. I had a massive heart attack that severely damaged the heart muscle. The LAD artery, commonly referred to as the widow maker artery, was ninety-five percent blocked, and I was minutes away from death. A stent was inserted to restore blood flow, but the heart attack had damaged my heart to a functioning capacity of only twenty percent.

The atmosphere in the room was intense. The doctors had left, but my condition was becoming unstable. My blood pressure shot up, my pulse was faint but rapid, and my breathing was extremely labored. It's difficult to articulate the depth of fear that I was experiencing. It was as if I could feel my soul leaving my body. My youngest daughter, Ashley, walked into the room and said she felt a spirit of death hovering over me and encouraged everyone to pray. My oldest daughter, who always takes charge, was rallying the nurses saying, "Somebody, do something. My mom can't breathe." Nervously, Cary was pacing in and out of the room.

The nurses were feverishly working to stabilize me. As my state of agitation increased, I fought to get a breath of air, and my chest felt like there was a monster inside me trying to force his way out. The pain was excruciating. Nurses gave me more morphine and increased my oxygen. The tension was palpable.

Some close friends began to arrive to show support. They had just returned from burying one of our close friends of more than thirty years, and now they were looking at me and wondering if I would be next. Pastor Ken and his wife, Laura, came in. Laura took one look at me and ran to the back of the room sobbing. I heard her say, "No, I can't take anymore." I cried out to God to forgive me for everything I had done to disappoint Him in my life. I questioned, is this the way my life will end?

By now our dear friends Dennis and Delores Barnes had come to see me. I began to say my goodbyes and profess my love for everyone. I told Dennis and Ken that I wanted them to sing at my funeral. Ken, sensing the urgency of the situation, leaned down and gently kissed my forehead, and proclaimed, "Remember, Dell, you will live and not die." These words gave me comfort and hope. Little did I know that the words spoken to me three days earlier would sustain me in my crucial hour of need.

The next five days were very difficult. My body was frail, and I felt sick and despondent. I wondered why God had let me live only to be incapacitated. Cary never left my side. He slept in a chair beside me every night. The doctor didn't know if the damaged part of my heart was dead or dormant. He said that if it were dormant, it would take many months, if not years, to gain any strength back, and there was no way of knowing when or if there would be any improvement. He warned me that my life would be different than I had known it to be in the past. He encouraged me to enjoy every day because I was a walking miracle and fortunate to be alive. He said that ninety percent of the people who experienced this kind of heart attack never made it to the hospital. I had, indeed, dodged a bullet. I knew my life would never be the same.

After days in the hospital, my condition stabilized enough to be discharged. My heart was so weak that I was fitted with a portable defibrillator in case I went into cardiac arrest. They informed me that I had to wear it 24/7...just in case. My doctor said I shouldn't be left alone in the event of another heart event. Cary, as always, was there to meet my every need. Because I was weak and out of breath, I was confined to bed most of the time. Every time I had a small ache or pain I wondered if I was having another heart attack. I became needier than ever, and I wanted my family with me constantly.

I surveyed my life and made sure all my relationships were intact. Although I was thankful to be alive, I wondered how my new life would look. Would I always feel so sick and weak? The medicines made me feel worse and more than likely added to my inability to cope which had deteriorated to the point of despair. Fear was my constant companion, and it engulfed me. God had done so many miraculously things in the past for me and had brought me through many challenges, yet I found myself at this point of hopelessness. I knew I desperately needed His touch in my life once again.

Three weeks had passed, and I was still very ill and depressed. One night a friend of my daughter called and said he had notified Pastor Rodney Howard Brown, a well-known Pastor in Brandon, Florida, to inform him of my condition. How our paths had crossed twenty years earlier will be revealed as my story unfolds. Pastor Rodney encouraged him to have me meet him at his church the following Sunday at 9:30 a.m. He declared God would heal me if I came. Somehow I knew I had to get there no matter how difficult it was.

Sunday morning I arrived at his church promptly at 9:30 a.m. with all my family. When the service began, Pastor Rodney summoned my family and me to come forward for prayer. They helped me to the front where Pastor Rodney began to pray. As he placed his hand on my forehead, I felt a surge of power like an electric shock shoot through my body.

Simultaneously my defibrillator siren issued a loud warning to stand back and call 911. I had only twenty seconds to deactivate the defibrillator before the shock would be issued to restart my heart, and I nervously deactivated the machine just in time. Pastor Rodney asked, "What just happened?" Everyone in the congregation was praying, alarmed by the sound of the siren. My family took me home from the service. Although I was still weak with no visible sign of healing, I knew God had touched me.

The very next day I had a follow-up doctor's appointment with my Cardiologist. During our visit, I told him about my experience and asked him to give me another test to check the strength of my heart. He looked at me like I was a little crazy. He refused, stating there hadn't been enough time since my heart attack to see any improvement. I respectfully reminded him that his timing and God's were not necessarily the same. He continued by saying that insurance wouldn't cover the cost and prematurely administering the test would only discourage me. I was persistent and told him we would cover the cost ourselves and demanded to have the test. Apparently, he had no idea how persistent I could be.

After bantering back and forth, the doctor finally gave in and agreed to do the echocardiogram, and three days later they performed the test. He promised to call as soon as he received the results. It was a long weekend of waiting, but on Monday, the doctor called. He asked if I was sitting down and stated that I must know someone upstairs. He reported that my heart was back in the normal range! Overflowing with gratitude at this news, I danced and screamed with pure joy. He said, "Take that defibrillator off and stomp it because you no longer need it. You have received another miracle." Glory to God for He had touched me!

Euphoria overcame me, and I knew I could not waste the new life given me. I promised God I would proclaim His goodness and mercy by sharing my story with a grateful heart, a brand new heart. I knew my life was spared for such a time as this. My purpose and mission were clear! Therefore, I must write, and write with confidence that my words will be guided by the One who gave me new life...let the journey begin!!!

Chapter 2

Apple of My Father's Eye

As I look back over the past sixty-five years, it's hard to count the numerous times I have asked God to erase the memories that have haunted me for so long. Ironically, I now find myself calling on Him to help me recall the details which have been buried in the deepest recesses of my mind. I realize that God allowed me to forget so I could be healed, and I am remembering now so others can be healed.

The first seven years of my life were much like that of any other child. I grew up in a small town in Tennessee to wonderful parents who adhered to basic Christian philosophy. My parents wanted more children, but after three pregnancies that ended in miscarriages, I was destined to be an only child. As an only child, I was showered with love and affection, but I longed for a sibling to share my childhood.

Mom was a typical woman of the Fifties, content with being a housewife. Dad was a very ambitious, hardworking man whose sole purpose was to provide a nice, comfortable life for his family. After a few years, dad's dream came true when he purchased a home by a lake on the outskirts of town. It was a small two-bedroom brick home, but it was a mansion to us.

My earliest memories were of mom baking cookies, dad riding me on his shoulders, picnics at the local State Park, fishing at the lake behind our house, attending church in the country, a one-room schoolhouse and Sunday dinners at my grandparent's house. Life was simple and unpretentious with a special emphasis on family values.

I was, you might say, the apple of my father's eye. He was very proud of his petite, blonde-haired, blue-eyed little girl and delighted in showing me off to his friends and relatives. Since I was on constant exhibition, I was expected to be the best at everything I tried. My father was my hero, and I endured tremendous pressure to make sure I never disappointed him. Mother was always there in a role of defender and protector. They often argued because she felt my dad was too strict and overbearing on me. I remember mother telling me of the horror she experienced when my dad tossed me off the pier in Savannah, Georgia, in an attempt to teach me to swim. Although I was a baby, barely old enough to walk, dad's theory was that my natural instincts would abound and I would swim to avoid drowning. This was a technique he observed while serving in the Navy, but of course, these were grown men in training. His theory was unproven, of course, with a small child; and he immediately realized he had to jump in and rescue me. Well, needless to say, my mother was very upset with my father and a precedent had been set for the years to come.

Dad worked for a bank in the city of Nashville. He was in charge of repossessing automobiles that were in default, and his job often required traveling out of town. One night mom and I were home alone, and around midnight we were awakened when the telephone rang. We've all experienced that surge of adrenalin that comes when the phone rings late at night, and we're overcome with the fear that something has happened to someone we love.

Our fears quickly came to a reality when we discovered my father had been in a severe automobile accident coming home from a nearby town. He was driving through a rural community when he fell asleep at the wheel and drove the car headlong into a rock bluff. He was thrown from the vehicle on impact and landed in the middle of the road. Ironically, a truck that was driven by my father's own cousin nearly struck him as he lay there seriously injured. His cousin recognized him, ran to the nearest farmhouse and called an ambulance. He notified mom and me at the same time. Because of the great distance he was from the nearest hospital, it took quite a long time for him to receive medical treatment. Of course, we drove as fast as we could and actually reached the hospital before the ambulance arrived. It seemed like an eternity before we reached the emergency room. I still remember that night like it was yesterday. Mom tried to be brave for me, but I sensed it was serious. My heart was racing, I could hardly breathe, and I trembled with fear. Even at the tender age of seven, I cried out to God, "Please help my daddy."

We had been in the waiting room for only a few minutes when the ambulance arrived. I broke away from my mom and ran to my dad as they were wheeling him into the emergency room. The horror of what I saw that night has haunted me my entire life. My dad was lying in a pool of blood. Deep lacerations in his head exposed his skull, and blood completely covered his entire face and body. Surely this wasn't my daddy! He regained consciousness and was crying out for me. He kept yelling, "Where is my arm? I can't feel my arm."

Mom and the nurses pulled me away as I fought and screamed to be close to my dad. I was frightened I would never see him again. The night seemed endless as we paced the floor waiting for news of his condition, but finally, we were told the extent of his injuries. He had multiple lacerations to his head requiring hundreds of stitches, and he had lost a tremendous amount of blood, but in actuality, those injuries were easily healed.

The most severe injuries were to his spine because all the nerves leading from his spinal column to his left arm had been severed leaving his left arm paralyzed. Soon after the injury, doctors determined the arm had to be amputated. My dad was in constant pain and torment. He described the pain as feeling like his arm was lying in a pit of unquenchable fire. The pain he endured was so horrible that he often prayed to die.

Dad was hospitalized for weeks. I could hardly wait to see him. I remember the day he came home after having his arm removed. The excitement of his return was quickly diminished when I looked at him. I was so young and impressionable that seeing the wound left me nauseated. For a period of time, I was even frightened of his disfigurement.

The scars on his head and face were healed, but they had changed his looks. Yes, my handsome dad had been changed. However, the most visible change was his countenance. He looked defeated and sad and maybe even embarrassed. I was too young to know what really was going on with my dad, but he came home a different person physically and emotionally. The confident, driven dad that I knew and loved was gone forever.

My Dad and I

My Mom and I

Chapter 3

Something to Cry About

The years that followed were filled with heartache and hardship for all of us. Dad had seven different spinal surgeries to eliminate his pain, and yet each surgery left him disabled in another way and did nothing to ease his pain. There were times I felt his emotional pain was almost worse than his physical pain. You see, my dad would not accept anything less than perfection, and he saw himself as imperfect and unable to perform as a whole person. In his opinion, his manhood had been compromised.

His disability left him unable to work, so mother took it upon herself to provide for us. She had never worked outside the home, and so she was forced to accept a menial job in a shirt factory sewing buttons on shirts. It was arduous work, but it provided the necessities in our time of need. As I look back on those years, I realize that mom suffered in her own way as much as my father. It wasn't as apparent because her pain was all internal. She had been pulled from a comfortable lifestyle and thrown into a situation of responsibility for which she was unprepared.

Although my parents did the best they could to make my life enjoyable, all the stress had a significant impact on me. I basically had to take on the responsibilities of an adult. Since my mother worked long hours and my father was disabled, I took on many of the duties of the home as well as trying to maintain my grades in school. I cooked, cleaned and tried to take care of my dad as best I could. Oh, don't misunderstand, I wasn't abused or at least I didn't feel abused. My parents loved me and tried to provide a happy life for me. Mom was completely self-sacrificing to make sure I always had the best she could provide, but life in my home was stressful and painful. It was difficult hearing my dad crying out in pain and hearing him beating his head against the wall in despair. In dad's eyes, living made dying look easy.

Mom did all she could, but the strain was wearing her down as well. Dad was often cruel to mom and me, but she always dismissed his behavior and said, "Dell, you know your dad is sick, and he doesn't mean to hurt us." I found no comfort in her reasoning. Dad had turned into an unreasonable, overbearing man full of bitterness, and we became the victims of his suffering.

Even though dad was in tremendous pain, he tried to take an active part in my life. I suppose his own disability plunged him even further into wanting me to excel in everything I did. He was trying to live out his dreams and his life through me. I know he loved me, but it was a selfish love that strangled the life out of me. If I failed, he considered it a personal failure for himself. Initially, he responded to my failures by withdrawing his affections, but later his responses became overt and belligerent. I felt like I could never measure up to his expectations, and it left me feeling depressed and insecure.

Dad had been on the Underwater Demolition Team (UDT) in the Navy during World War II. This group later became known as the Seal Team known for its fierceness and skill in battle. My dad was fearless. Because of his training and background in the Navy, he was an accomplished swimmer and diver. Naturally, he wanted me to become a champion athlete in water sports, but frankly, I didn't have the ability. During the summer, he helped out at the State Park teaching swimming lessons. I was a pretty good swimmer, but my fear of heights prohibited me from becoming a good diver. I remember one day very vividly.

All my friends were having fun at the park, and dad decided I was going to dive off the twenty-foot board. I can still remember trembling as I climbed up the ladder and walked to the end of the board. As I stood there looking down at him, he looked so tiny in the water. He kept yelling, "You can do it. Make daddy proud," but I just kept pleading, "Don't make me dad, I'm scared." He responded with, "You big baby. Dive or I'll give you something to cry about." He was obviously embarrassed that I had humiliated him as he put me on display. Realizing the only way I was getting down was to dive, I gathered all the courage I could and took the plunge. Before I hit the water, I lifted my head which caused me to hit the water in a flattened position. I suppose falling from that height was like falling off a two-story building and landing on my stomach. Needless to say, the impact temporarily knocked me out, but there were no serious injuries, at least not to my body.

When I gained consciousness, I looked at my dad and screamed and told him I hated him, and I guess at that moment, I did. He had humiliated me in front of my friends. He hurt me and betrayed the trust that I held so sacred. Forgiving him was hard. He blamed me for my failed attempt and said I was weak. To him, fear was not an option for me, and yet I believe his fear was greater than mine. The fear of his own inability to perform and succeed became his greatest disability.

This was only one incident where my dad's expectation of me was unreasonable. On another occasion, he bought me a small horse. His intentions were good. He knew how much I loved horses, and he wanted to surprise me for my birthday. It was a day I will never forget in more than one way. I couldn't wait to climb on her back and go for a ride; but as soon as I mounted her, she took off in a wild gallop. Try as I might, I could not stop her. She ran through trees, bushes, fences and anything else in her path. After what seemed to be an eternity, the horse threw me in a thorn-filled bush leaving me with deep scratches and bruises. Dad cleaned me up and then demanded that I get up and try again. Begging and pleading for a reprieve did nothing to sway him. He threatened me with a belt and belittled me saying, "Get back on that horse you big baby, or I'll give you something to cry about. You can ride until you quit crying." Fear turned to hate, and the resentment toward my dad grew each day as he continually pressured me to be something I could not be. There's a fine line between love and hate, and I bounced back and forth in those emotions like a rubber ball.

During these years, every day seemed to present a new challenge. There were financial pressures, and the stress and pain of my father's illness seemed unbearable. His intolerance of my fears and failures was increasing day by day until his threats came to fruition. He began to spank me with his belt out of total frustration. In a rage, mom threatened to kill him if he hit me again. Ironically, she had no problem spanking me herself and even made me find the stick she would beat me with. Sadly, this scene became commonplace.

My Dad after his amputation

Chapter 4

The Hiding Place

Each surgery dad went through to relieve his pain seemed to be a life and death situation, and yet nothing could alleviate his torment. Doctors kept him heavily sedated, and as a result, his body became addicted to the drugs. It seemed as though the only time he wasn't experiencing pain was when he was sleeping and the only way he could sleep was to anesthetize himself. We went through the same routine night after night. Mom would go to bed tired from her mundane job. Dad would take his pills and fall asleep in his chair. I would wake up realizing dad wasn't in bed, awaken mom, and together we would drag his limp and heavy body to the bedroom so he could rest more comfortably.

There were times when my father's nakedness would be exposed as he slept. I was only a child, but I can vividly remember the confused feelings I had. Dad was a proud man and would have been mortified had he known that I was able to see him in his vulnerability, but I always kept it a secret. Mom must have known, but we never discussed it. Sometimes I felt guilty because I would think about seeing my dad in that way. As I approached adolescence, curiosity would creep into my thoughts, and the guilt would consume me. Although these were completely innocent encounters, they left deep emotional scars on me. I would always try to cover him as not to humiliate him further, but the sorrow and guilt followed me.

I didn't know much about sex, but I did understand that it was not a part of my parents' life. Many nights I would hear my parents crying across the hall, and I would cover my ears and sing into my pillow so I couldn't hear the sounds. I thought to myself that sex must be an awful experience. Dad's disabilities had rendered him impotent. Because of his impotence, he became extremely insecure and often accused mom of cheating on him. He would yell and curse at her, belittling her unmercifully. His insecurities transferred into further abusiveness. It was so unfair to treat her in this way. All mom ever did was work and take care of dad and me. She would take his insults and accusations for only so long and then she would retaliate. Our once loving home had become a house with three dysfunctional, hurting people. I wanted so desperately to run away, but I had nowhere to go.

Dad was a heavy smoker, and often he would fall asleep with a cigarette in his hand. Having no feeling in his left side, he would frequently burn himself badly as he slept. On one such occasion, I was awakened by the smell of smoke and quickly ran to the den where I found my father sitting in a burning chair with his pants on fire. Mom heard me screaming and came running. We beat the flames out and dressed his burns. It could have had a disastrous outcome if I had not been awakened by the smell of smoke. Fear, tension, sorrow, anger and confusion were my constant companions. Was I the only little girl in the world who had to live like this?

It was ironic that although my father was disabled, unemployed and in constant pain, he managed to think of others and did what he could to help those in need. He would go out and find hitchhikers and bring them home for a good meal and a shower. They would often stay for extended periods of time. It's hard to imagine how dangerous it could have been, but it was a different time back then. He frequently gave mom's hard-earned money to the needy. Mom couldn't help resenting him for putting the needs of others before our own and showing more kindness to them than he gave to us. Everyone loved my dad. He was Mr. Personality to the outside world, but mom and I had a different perspective. I suppose he felt it was safe to let down his defenses with us which made it even harder to accept.

I remember one day at school I had gone to the restroom and one of my classmates came in after me. Lucille came from a very poor family and was slow to learn. She was wearing a skirt that was made merely of fabric taken from a bolt of material wrapped around her body and pinned with a safety pin. She had no lunch or school supplies. That evening I told my dad how sad I felt for her, and that was all it took. We took food and clothing to them. Upon arriving, we discovered they had no coal for their furnace and no furniture except food crates. Dad took it upon himself to provide for them and share whatever we had. I learned so much from those experiences even though it caused a lot of heated battles at home. My dad was a good man in many ways, with a big heart. I wonder what our lives would have been like if he had not had that terrible accident that left him in constant pain and turmoil.

In spite of these momentary reprieves from the chaos, I couldn't help but question why I was being robbed of the joy of my youth? Why didn't God answer my prayers and heal my dad so we could be a normal family? Maybe it was because my faith wasn't strong enough, or perhaps it was because I was a bad girl and God was punishing me. Was it my fault dad was so ill? There were so many unanswered questions, but I did know it was much too heavy a load for a little girl to carry. There were so many times when I echoed dad's prayers to die with him. Life seemed hopeless. Would I ever be happy?

When the days became too difficult for me to cope, I would go to a special hiding place I found at the lake behind our house. There was a large boulder, hidden by the trees where I would sit, think about my life and skip stones on the water. It was a place of solace and peace where no one could find me. I imagined myself sitting at the feet of Jesus and laying my head on his lap as He gently stroked my brow. I imagined Him telling me how much He loved me. It gave me the strength to go back and face life again. The vision I encountered at the rock by the lake became my comfort, not only then, but for years to come.

I can't help but think today of the countless numbers of lost individuals who wake up each morning facing dismal situations not unlike what I experienced – hopeless and alone. Their only hope is a loving heavenly Father who will carry them along to the other side of their pain.

Chapter 5

A Lesson to Remember

In addition to being a friend to the friendless, dad became a consummate crusader. During those years when racial prejudice had run rampant in the south, dad had pioneered some of the first sit-ins in our small town. He stood in the gap for equal rights which was very unpopular in our area. He, like many other whites, believed in equal rights for everyone but held to separation as it related to interracial relationships.

Many children in the south were raised by black nannies, and I was no exception. My nanny's name was Hattie Mae. She was a large-framed black woman who loved me like her own and affectionately referred to me as child. I can close my eyes and still see Hattie standing at the ironing board singing praises to God and speaking in some kind of gibberish. I listened intently, and with childlike inquisitiveness, I questioned, "Hattie, what are you saying? Are you speaking African?" "No child, I'm just talking to the Lord."

Her faith was evident, and she was relentless in trying to instill her faith in me. I was completely unaware at my tender age that Hattie was introducing me to Pentecost. As far back as my memory will take me, I can see God's hand on me in preparation to write this book.

As I grew to be a preteen, my dad became aware of a young black teenage boy named Samuel. He came from a poor family and had little opportunity to succeed. Samuel had a very obvious speech impediment and stuttered severely, and even though he had a lot to overcome, my dad saw great potential in him.

At the time, we owned a dry cleaning business, and even though the income was meager, it was a way to provide income for the family. My mom and dad became surrogate parents to Samuel and mentored him in the business. Dad taught him so much and, of course, always demanded Samuel's best. He was a huge help to my mom and dad. My dad loved Samuel, and so did I.

Prejudice had a stronghold in our area. Dad often discovered that Samuel was being mistreated, and this made his blood boil. On one occasion, dad and I were walking through town on our way to lunch, and we ran into Samuel. My dad asked Samuel to come along with us. Samuel said, "No, no, Mr. Porter. I can't do that." My dad insisted and encouraged Samuel to join us.

We entered the small restaurant and walked to the counter with Samuel nervously walking behind us. Samuel joined us as we sat down. The owner, who was a friend of my dad, came and asked what Samuel was doing there. My dad said, "He's hungry, and we invited him to join us for lunch." The owner said, "We don't serve his kind here," as he placed his shotgun on the counter. Nervously, I asked my dad if we could leave. He told me to be quiet, and he continued the dialogue with the owner. My dad reminded the owner of their long-time friendship and told him, "If you plan on shooting someone, you can shoot me first." He firmly added, "Put the gun away and fix us something to eat." My dad knew no fear, but Samuel and I were scared to death.

After a lengthy confrontation, we were served our lunch, all three of us, and I walked out like a proud peacock. Samuel stuttered a little worse that day, and I learned a valuable lesson that I would never forget. As we left the restaurant, my dad said, "Dell, always stand up for what you believe is right." I looked at him with pride and said, "I will daddy, I promise."

Today Samuel owns his own business in Tennessee and is very successful. When I go home to my hometown, I include a stop to see my old friend and fondly remember our connection.

Chapter 6

Trying to Measure Up

The pain and sickness my father endured over the years eventually took a toll on his heart. At age thirty-five, he had his first heart attack, and I thought for sure that it was the end. Dad was hospitalized, and doctors began to wean him off the narcotics on which he had become dependent. The withdrawals that resulted were so intense that he would have to be strapped to the bed as he screamed from the tormenting pain and hallucinations.

At times, he was so uncontrollable that mom picked me up from school and took me to the hospital to try to keep him calm. I crawled up in his bed and held him very close, and he began to calm down. "I love you, dad. Everything will be okay. I'm here, dad."

I felt like the parent-child roles had been reversed in our family. As a child, wasn't I the one supposed to be held and comforted? I desperately needed to feel protected and nurtured, but all I felt was loneliness and fear.

Even though I had a difficult home life and lived in a dysfunctional family, there were many bright spots. I was an excellent student. After all, my dad wouldn't accept anything less. He expected me to be the best, and my grades reflected my desire to make him proud. I was very active in school and had many good friends. I was always the life of the party because I felt an obligation to make people laugh so that they would accept me. I've often heard it said that people who masquerade as clowns are merely trying to cover the pain they feel inside, and I was a good example of that theory.

Probably the brightest spot in my childhood was my friendship with my best friend, Sandy. She and I were inseparable and shared a common bond. Her father was alcohol dependent, and consequently, our lives were similar in many ways. We didn't talk a lot about our problems, but we knew that we shared a bond that would endure time and space which it has.

When life seemed too unbearable, I would run to Sandy because I knew she would make me laugh and forget what was going on at home. She always seemed stronger than me, invincible to her own pain. I thank God for Sandy and how she helped me through some very difficult years. She became the sister I never had.

Two years passed, and dad was back in the hospital with a second heart attack. We went through the usual trauma of not knowing whether he would survive or not. I knew in my heart that dad would have peace only after death, and many times I realized that only then would mom and I find peace. Heaven and hell were not a reality to me at that age. I knew about God, we even went to church, but Christ was not the center of our lives. The only peace I have today about my dad is the belief in my heart that he is with Jesus and not suffering anymore. I cannot bear the thought that he is still in torment. Although I don't know for sure, I choose to believe that dad made his peace with the Lord and that he is enjoying himself as a whole person once again.

The doctors told us that dad was not strong enough to survive a third heart attack, and we tried to prepare ourselves for that day. Dad was still hospitalized with his second heart attack but was recovering rapidly. One night when mom and I were visiting with him, it began to snow. Dad cautioned us that the roads would be getting slick, and we should head for home. As we were leaving, he asked mom to leave the room so he could speak to me alone. I sat on the edge of his bed, and he told me how much he loved me and how sorry he was for all he had put me through. He asked me to forgive him for all the hurt he had caused me. Then he made a very strange request. He asked me to go home and find the suit that mom and I had given him for Christmas and get it cleaned. I asked him why, and all he said was that he would need it.

Dad proceeded to tell me to be strong, to help mom and to be his little soldier. He said, "Don't worry, I'll be fine." In my heart, I knew he was saying goodbye. He also made me promise that I would wait until I married to give myself to anyone and to always conduct myself in a way that would make him proud. I promised that I would, told him I loved him and kissed him goodbye. More importantly, I told him I forgave him. My words were empty as it took many years to fully realize the pain I had suffered and to understand what real forgiveness looks like. It was finally over. God had answered dad's prayers, as the scripture says, "For he has not despised or scorned the suffering of the afflicted one; he has not hidden his face from him but has listened to his cry for help." (Psalm 22:24)

I was only fifteen when he died, and I felt as if a part of me had died with him. For months I ran the gambit of emotions: loneliness, anger, abandonment, fear of not being needed, guilt, resentment and grief beyond belief. All these emotions later transferred into teenage rebellion and a life-long search for significance to appease the void he had left.

In my father's persistence to create perfection in me, he left me with a legacy – always be the best you can be and never settle for second best. I know these are good qualities when kept in perspective, but fear of my father's rejection if I failed to be the best had set a pattern for my entire life. I felt that if I weren't the best, people wouldn't like or accept me, and rejection would lead to abandonment. The fear of failure became the motivating force in everything I did. What's more, my desire to be needed became the precept for becoming a self-imposed Florence Nightingale to everyone.

As a Christian, I have struggled with the idea that I would dishonor my father's memory by being honest about his wrong behavior toward mom and me. Philippians 3:13b-14 says, "Forgetting what is behind and straining toward what is ahead, I press on toward the goal to win the prize for which God has called me heavenward in Christ Jesus."

I felt confused that this meant forgetting the past entirely, but over time I came to realize I couldn't forgive what I couldn't remember. It was impossible for me to accept healing for a wound I denied receiving.

I refuse to justify any further my dad's harshness, and yes, even his cruelty at times toward me, but I can't deny the good qualities he possessed either. He suffered greatly, and unfortunately, mom and I suffered with him.

For most of my life, I lived in denial that dad had ever hurt me physically, but recently the memory of the physical cruelty resurfaced. I had remembered only what I could afford to live with; but Jesus said, "Then you will know the truth, and the truth will set you free." (John 8:32)

It has taken many years, but facing my relationship with my father honestly has allowed me to admit the extent of his influence on me. My own ideals and hunger for a nurturing father blinded me to his shortcomings. He gave his conditional love based on my performance and achievements, and this had made it difficult for me to comprehend the unconditional love of my loving heavenly Father. Although the journey back has been painful, it opened the door for complete forgiveness and the freedom to grow into the woman that God intended me to be.

Chapter 7

The Cowboy

Dawn was breaking on March 5, 1964, the day my dad was to be buried. I lay awake all night clutching one of his worn t-shirts still fragrant from his Old Spice cologne. There was no comfort as I reflected on thoughts of my daddy and how his illness had robbed us of a happy life. Dad was only thirty-seven years old. He was a good man who loved his family, but his pain and suffering had changed him. The entire dynamics of our family changed the night he fell asleep while driving home.

I heard a pitter-patter on my window and peeked through the curtains to find a light snow falling. It was late in the season for snow; but as I watched the snow falling so peacefully, I realized spring was just around the corner. The last snow of the season seemed symbolic that the winter of our lives was over and that there was a new beginning about to take place for mom and me.

Mom and I would have to pick up the tattered remnants of our lives and begin again. Fortunately, dad had a small $10,000 life insurance policy. Mom realized she had to better herself and leave the drudgery of the shirt factory, so she used the policy funds to enroll in a school of cosmetology.

We used the small balance of the money to survive that year until mom could get a job to support us.

Losing dad was devastating. I thought my heart would shatter into a thousand pieces, but I had to admit that I didn't miss the strain of seeing him suffer any longer. I suppose I was even a tiny bit relieved that his suffering was over. In retrospect, I believe mom tried to overcompensate for the difficult years we experienced by becoming very lenient and allowing me to do most anything I wanted to do. Or, perhaps she just checked out of parenting me at a crucial time in my life because she had her own pain to deal with and was tired, very tired of the stress and heartache. It was her turn to thrive. Certainly, she loved me, but showing her love was overshadowed by her determination to make something of her life.

I was fifteen years old and, like most teenagers, I was happiest when I was surrounded by friends, especially Sandy. She was my rock, I loved her like a sister, and we were together constantly. Growing up in a small town had its challenges. Our small town didn't offer a lot of options for entertainment, but we were creative in our quest for fun. We never felt like we were missing out. In fact, we felt privileged.

The big event of the week was cruising the local drive-in on Friday night. The Tasty Mug was a drive-in hamburger joint which served as the local hangout for teenagers. It was crowded bumper-to-bumper every weekend with cars circling and everyone searching for familiar faces. The Friday night run was considered a success if it resulted in getting asked out on a date for Saturday night.

One night as Sandy and I were cruising after a big football game, we went to the Mug for a burger and ran into a carload of guys from Austin Peay State College. They were local guys and considerably older, so we had never hung out together. However, I had an immediate connection with one of the guys named Luke. He was charismatic, charming, and the fact that he was a drummer in a pop band made him a hot commodity.

Luke and I started dating, and before long we were going steady. Mom was concerned about the four-year difference in our ages. She felt he might lead me astray because he was more experienced. Luke was my first love, I was crazy about him, but I never wavered on my promise to my father the night he died.

The Sixties were very turbulent years for everyone. The Viet Nam war had begun, the drug culture was escalating, and great leaders were being assassinated. I will never forget sitting in history class and hearing the principal announce over the intercom that President John F. Kennedy had been assassinated. What was the world coming to? Our future seemed uncertain. As the war escalated, the tragedy of war began to strike our town with a vengeance. Friends were wounded and killed in battle with an overwhelming frequency, and it had a profound impact on everyone in our community. We found solace in each other and shared a common bond of fear and loss.

Luke was getting worried. His grades were failing in school, and he knew he ran the risk of being drafted. One day he came to me and said he decided to join the Navy to avoid the draft. He knew being drafted would almost certainly buy him a ticket to Viet Nam where he would be involved in a ground war. He was my first love, and my heart was broken. I couldn't believe he was leaving me. A break-up was inevitable.

As usual, Sandy was there to comfort me. Every weekend we rallied friends together to create a new adventure. These adventures were as varied and crazy as the imagination of the kids who dreamed them up. Cave exploring, climbing the water towers and writing graffiti on them, frog gigging, snipe hunting and horse shows were some of our staple things to do. Basically, the event was not as important as just being together with friends. We were all good kids just looking for laughs and for a good time. There was very little crime back then, so we had the freedom to explore our youth.

My home was a favorite place to hang out. We were one of the first families to have a color television which further enhanced the desire to hang out at our house. Every Wednesday night a group of friends gathered to watch Hullabaloo and Shindig. Mom enjoyed my friends as much as I did and was always great about preparing snacks and joining in the fun.

Our home overlooked a ten-acre lake, and our friends enjoyed coming over to go fishing and do other activities around the lake. We had a large basement that we set up as a party room. Truthfully, there was a continuous flow of friends in and out of our home, and many happy memories were made there. As a teenager, I was in constant motion. In the summer months, we were either swimming at the State Park or hanging out at the pool at a nearby cave.

During the winter we lived for snow days when school was closed. We loved snow sledding at the golf course, hayrides, skating on the frozen lake behind our house and building bonfires. At least once a week we all gathered at the drive-in movie. We were challenged to see how many people we could cram in the car or sneak in hidden in the trunk. Sitting out on the hood of the car laughing and having fun was more important than watching the movie. Some of the best times were riding our horses to the drive-in. We brought blankets to sit on while we watched the film out under the stars. It was a time of innocence, a time of escape from the tragedies of war and uncertainty. They were the best of times and the worst of times, times of laughter and times of tears.

One very memorable experience happened after a football game. About a hundred kids went to the city dump for a victory celebration after defeating a school rival. A huge bonfire was built as we all cheered and enjoyed our conquest. There was a dilapidated shed nearby that looked private enough for a potty break. I walked over to it with a girlfriend and heard the cries of five little kittens that seemed to be abandoned. I gathered up the kittens and headed back to the crowd. All the girls were oohing and aahing over the kittens when one of the guys on the football team grabbed one of the kittens and ran to the fire. He yelled over and over, "We're going to have a sacrifice! We're going to have a sacrifice!" I was mortified as I saw him toss the kitten into the fire. Screaming and yelling, I tried to fight him off as he came for more. I stuffed the kittens up my blouse hoping to deter him, but he was unaffected. As I screamed for help, some of the guys came to my aid and grabbed him and threatened to throw him in the fire. One of those guys was Rex, someone I had known for many years.

Rex was a real-life cowboy who lived on a ranch and was a skilled horseman who rode in horse shows and rodeos every week. In fact, my dad hired him to break the first horse that he bought me. I never liked him very much because he always teased and made fun of me, but that night Rex became my hero. I gathered the kittens up and headed for home. Sandy was at my house for a sleepover and was waiting for me with my mom. It was past my curfew, so they were worried and were on the verge of calling the police. We didn't have cell phones back then so there was no way to let them know I would be late. I wasn't about to leave those kittens with that maniac! With kittens under my shirt, I headed home. My mom was furious because I violated my curfew and even more angry that I brought the kittens home with me. What a night it had been!

That night opened the door for the beginning of a relationship with Rex, and we began to date casually. Rex was a lot of fun and very popular in school. His family owned the Tasty Mug, the local hangout for teenagers, and also Freddie's Restaurant. Freddie's was an all-night truck stop near the local drive-in theater and another place to hang out in town. His family actually monopolized the entertainment in our area.

What a great time we had together. We rode horses every weekend, and I began to travel to horse shows with Rex's family. One summer they invited me to go with them to a month-long trail ride in the Ozark Mountains. What a blast it was camping out, bathing in the river, chuck wagons, square dancing, campfires and loving life in the outdoors. It was such a carefree lifestyle, and I loved it.

Rex was always ready for a good time. Our relationship started out carefree and frivolous which was a welcome departure from my home life. Rex wasn't a very good student, so when he graduated from high school he decided college was not an option for him. Once again the fear of Viet Nam loomed over our heads, and it plagued every young man I knew. That summer after his graduation our relationship escalated. Things were definitely getting serious between us and passions were running high, but still, the promise I made to my dad would keep things in check physically.

As the weeks and months passed, the reality of being drafted became more and more inevitable. Rex was encouraged to see an Army recruiter who convinced him to enlist. By enlisting, or so he was told, he could avoid the draft and be guaranteed to be stationed in some exotic post where he would receive specialized training and education. Well, it seemed like a good plan. After all, he wanted to take advantage of every opportunity to ensure a secure future, and our town didn't offer a lot of opportunity for anyone. Unfortunately, it didn't come to fruition.

Rex enlisted in the Army, but two weeks after Advanced Infantry Training, he received his marching orders for Viet Nam. I will never forget the night he told me he was leaving. We held each other and cried, fearing we might never see each other again. I was almost eighteen years old. Too young to make a lifelong commitment, but I loved him and knew I didn't want to lose him. In thirty days he would be leaving, but we were together every moment we could steal. Confused and frightened, with so many thoughts going through our heads, we came to only one conclusion - marriage was the only way to share our love completely. I never forgot my promise to my dad.

They say hindsight is always twenty-twenty. Looking back I realize we married for all the wrong reasons. Rex wanted to make sure he had someone waiting for him, and

I wanted to quench my desire to be needed. I was on a constant search for significance. In my foolish naivety, I feared that if he were killed, I might live my whole life alone without love. I wanted to give myself to him entirely, but the fear and guilt of denying my father's dying request would have haunted me forever. After weighing all the options, we concluded that marriage was the best alternative. Oh, the follies of our youth. Unfortunately, my mom didn't make much of an effort to discourage me in my decision.

If I had only known the Lord then, I'm sure my decision would have been different, and my life would have had an entirely different outcome. Every choice we make impacts our lives and the lives of those we love. Without the Lord's guidance, we are left to make decisions on our own, and the consequences can be devastating. Proverbs 3:5-6 encourages, "Trust in the LORD with all your heart and lean not on your own understanding; in all your ways submit to him, and he will make your paths straight."

Chapter 8

A Casualty of War

Fear and desperation catapulted Rex and me into making a decision that we were ill-prepared to make. Our youth, inexperience and immaturity were a formula for disaster; but like most kids that age, we thought we had all the answers. As a young girl, I dreamed of a fairy-tale wedding complete with all the pomp and circumstance of a flowing white gown, a large wedding party in a beautiful church surrounded by friends and relatives to celebrate the joyous occasion. However, there was no way my mom could afford to fund the wedding of my dreams. Besides, there was no time to plan for a grand wedding.

Rex came home for a few days to discuss our wedding options. We were running out of ideas when he came up with a crazy plan. Since we were so involved with horses, he suggested we get married on horseback. With his logic, he convinced me it would be fun and inexpensive. One week later we invited a few friends to our wedding in an indoor arena near our home. In truth, it was a large barn, but indoor arena sounds better so I'll leave it at that. We were dressed in our finest western attire, a far departure from my dream of a white flowing gown. Of course, Sandy was my maid of honor. After a short ceremony, we were pronounced husband and wife, and my new husband whisked me off my horse and onto his. We literally rode off into the sunset together. Well, it sounds romantic, but looking back on the whole experience makes me laugh and blush with embarrassment.

How could we be so naïve? In reality, my husband was on his way to Viet Nam. Raging hormones, immaturity and total fear had prompted us to make a very foolish decision. Furthermore, where was my mother in all this? Her attempt to discourage me from such a foolish decision was weak at best. In later years, I resented her lack of trying to persuade me to make better choices, but sadly mom was so self-absorbed in her own pain that she inadvertently checked out of being a parent to me.

The honeymoon consisted of one night in a motel nearby, and the next day he had to return to his post. We had a few stolen moments before he shipped out to Viet Nam; and then, in the blink of an eye, he was gone.

Rex was deployed for thirteen months into a hell that could only be understood by the soldiers who shared the experience of war. Every night I sat glued to the television hoping to hear an update on his unit but soon realized that no news was considered good news. Letters kept my hopes alive for a while, but they started coming less and less often. The audio tapes we started sending to each other created more fear and anxiety as sounds of gunfire and explosions were overpowering his voice. Night after night I lay in bed wondering if I would become a widow at such a young age. Every morning I ran to the mailbox hoping to receive a letter or tape ensuring his safety. Tears soaked my pillow every night, and I wondered if the nightmare would ever end.

The time passed slowly, but his tour of duty finally came to an end, and it was time for him to return home. I realized he would be a different person, but I had no idea how deeply scarred he would be.

I worked at the local hospital while he was gone and saved enough money to put a small down payment on a mobile home. My excitement to see him again was undeniable. My heart felt like it would burst with excitement and pure elation; however, my joy was short-lived. My young husband left for Viet Nam as a fun loving, invincible young man, but he came back broken with a severe case of P.T.S.D. Was this the same person I married? The boy I loved came home a man I didn't know. The brutality of the war changed him. He was incapable of responsibility and showing love. He was nervous and jumped at every little noise. At times, he was hostile, and yet on other occasions, he sat and cried as he recalled images of fallen friends. Marijuana became his best friend. I tried to comfort him, but I wasn't equipped to handle the magnitude of his problems.

To further complicate matters, I became pregnant a couple of months after he returned home. My life was going from bad to worse. Rex became increasingly agitated with no ability to cope. The thoughts of being a father sent him completely over the edge, and one day he jumped on his motorcycle and took off across the country on a joy ride with another woman. The last thing he said was, "I'm not ready for this; I want a divorce." My dreams and my life were shattered.

Finding myself alone, pregnant and brokenhearted, I went back home again to my mother's house. To say I was miserable is a huge understatement. I became angry, bitter and terrified of what would become of my child and me. The pregnancy didn't go well, and I gave birth to a premature baby boy who weighed only three pounds. The struggle to keep him alive became the most important thing in my life. Fortunately, mom was supportive in every way. It was clear my life was going to change forever. Rex abandoned my newborn baby and me and checked out of our lives. With no real education, a sickly baby and a wounded spirit, I knew I was in serious trouble. By the time our son was a few months old, Rex and I were divorced.

Sandy had married her high school sweetheart about the same time Rex and I got married. Unfortunately, she wasn't any luckier in love than I was; and ironically, we found ourselves in divorce court on the same day. We found solace in our strong friendship and determined that we would always be there for each other. Little did I know my most difficult days were ahead of me.

Chapter 9

The Psychopath

After careful consideration, Sandy and I knew we had to leave our small-town environment if we were ever going to escape the memories of our past failures.   Overcoming the stigma of being divorced in a small town where everyone knew us would be impossible.   We knew the ghosts of our past would be encountered at every corner, plus we wanted to avoid being the subject of idle gossip.   We just wanted to blend into the culture, and there were just too many reminders of past hurts to allow us the ability to start a new life in our hometown.   I also knew that living in the same town with Rex and his family would be a convenient breeding ground for battles over our son, Cliff, and that was something I wanted to avoid at all costs.

Mom had been a blessing during the time we were fighting for Cliff's survival, but I wanted my independence from her as well.   I knew if I stayed, I would have to listen to her lecture on how to live my life, and I didn't want anyone telling me what to do.   I was naive and arrogant enough to think I had all the answers, but independence would come at a price.

We knew there were difficult times ahead, but we looked

forward to being on our own. The past was just that...the past, and we wanted to put it behind us. So, we set out on a quest to find true happiness and independence in the big city.

We packed the remnants of our failed marriages and headed to Nashville. After combining our furniture and household items, we had enough to fill a small, two-bedroom apartment with everything we needed. Two guys we went to high school with came over with a truck to help us move. It rained all day, but it didn't dampen our spirits for one minute. We were determined to pursue our dreams, and nothing was going to get in our way or delay us.

Although I was anxious to move out and live my own life, I must admit the thought of being a single parent at such a young age frightened me. I questioned my ability to accept the enormous responsibility of such a difficult task, but each time I expressed self-doubts, Sandy would reassure me by playfully saying, "Don't worry, Dell, you'll be the mommy, and I'll be the daddy. We can do anything as long as we're together." No one could have had a better friend. I knew I could always count on Sandy.

Both Sandy and I were fortunate enough to secure pretty good jobs. I landed a job at a bank in Printer's Alley as a switchboard operator making $325.00 a month, and Sandy was working as a secretary for an architect making about the same. After paying our car payments, rent and other fixed expenses, there was nothing left for anything else. We were living on a shoestring, but we were getting by.

Sometimes, when unforeseen expenses occurred, we wouldn't even have enough money to buy groceries. Many times we pooled our last few dollars together to have enough to buy formula and baby food for Cliff. We often resorted to sharing his food to keep from going hungry. The strained cherry cobbler was everyone's favorite, so we kept several jars on hand.

Times were definitely tough, but we didn't seem to mind. We managed to have fun even in the rough times. I guess, in a way, we were playing house, and Cliff was our little doll. He was the cutest baby in the world. Because he was premature, he was still very tiny and needed a lot of attention. He gave us a sense of belonging and purpose that we had never known. Sandy loved Cliff as much as I did and never once complained about sacrificing for a child that didn't belong to her. I could have never made it without her.

In the beginning, Sandy and I didn't know anyone, so we kept to ourselves just taking care of Cliff, but it didn't take long for us to accumulate some friends. The apartment complex was complete with a large swimming pool, and we enjoyed hanging out there. It was the social center for the complex and the place to meet new friends. We hadn't lived there too long when we met a nice young couple named Jim and Mallory. They seemed like the perfect couple. Jim was very handsome and definitely the more outgoing of the two. Mallory was beautiful but somewhat quiet. I really liked them both, but Sandy wasn't quite as taken with them as I was. I always thought Mallory was very fortunate to have such an attentive husband who showered her with love and affection. I wondered if I would ever have a relationship where I could love and be loved.

My strongest desire was to have a happy marriage and a good father for Cliff, but I felt those relationships only happened in the movies. I dreamed of being married to the perfect husband. I had fantasized about a house with a white picket fence around it and a big yard with a couple of kids running and playing in it. I suppose every young girl has her own idea of the perfect romantic and idealistic lifestyle with the man of her dreams. I dreamed, but I never thought my dreams would become a reality. After all, who would want to marry someone who had another man's child? I felt like I was considered used goods and felt completely unlovable.

Not long after we moved in, we met a new girlfriend who we affectionately called Gribble. Grib was a girl who marched to the tune of a different drummer. She was a real character and cute as a button. She was, without a doubt, the most carefree person in the world. She couldn't cook, but she could smell food cooking a mile away, and she'd come running. She lived to party and to have fun. Yes, Grib was definitely a party animal, and she tried her best to get Sandy and me to spread our wings. Grib's claim to fame was playing the role of motorcycle mama in a B-grade film. She'd do anything for shock factor. Sometimes she'd come over to our apartment with a stogie hanging out one corner of her mouth. She provided a lot of color to our somewhat dull lifestyle.

Our apartment was party central, and we were seldom alone. We took advantage of our new freedom and independence. Frankly, we were frivolous and acted irresponsibly and careless. Looking back, we had a lot of fun, but I, in truth, was really lonely. It's hard to imagine I could feel lonely when I was always surrounded by people, but it was a deeper, more penetrating loneliness. More than anything, I wanted a real home and family to share with someone I loved. There was such a void in my life. I felt like it could only be filled by a husband who would take care of Cliff and me.

Nearly every weekend, Sandy went home to her mother's. She was dedicated to her mom, and she was committed to her church. I admired her devotion, but I just couldn't see it for my own life. Sandy grew up in a strict Christian environment that had many restrictions attached, restrictions I could not accept. Besides, I didn't have a good track record with God. I felt that He had let me down when He didn't help my dad or heal my broken marriage. Although Cliff had survived against all the odds, I carried bitterness around that consumed me. I felt I must have been unworthy of God's love, or He would have helped when I called on Him. I guess I just didn't measure up in God's eyes. In fact, I envisioned God as a big bully ready to zap me each time I made a mistake. So, believing that God could fill the loneliness in my life was not a consideration.

When Sandy went out of town, I often took Cliff over to Jim and Mallory's for a visit. One day when I went to visit, Jim said that Mallory was ill and that I shouldn't bring the baby inside. I agreed and went back home. The next day I left Cliff with Sandy, and I went to see how Mallory was feeling. Jim was still at work, so Mallory answered the door. When she opened the door, I was shocked to see she had two black eyes. She immediately chuckled in a kind of nervous way and said she had been hit in the bridge of the nose by a golf ball while she and Jim were playing golf. It seemed like a reasonable explanation to me because I knew that Jim was an avid golfer. Although I believed her account, I felt like something was a little strange, and it made me uncomfortable. I decided it would be best if I didn't visit there for a while.

All the responsibilities of being a single parent were getting to me. There was a rebellion stirring inside of me that was beginning to take control. With a childhood undoubtedly filled with unwanted pressure and hardship and then marrying so young, I had never really sowed any wild oats and now seemed like as good a time as any. Grib was having too much fun for me not to take notice. I didn't need a lot of coaxing for the wild child in me to come out and play.

I started acting more and more irresponsibly by drinking and partying. A lot of our friends were getting into drugs, but my knowledge of what drugs had done to my father kept me from experimenting. I wanted no part of that scene at all, but I often stayed out late at night and then worked the next day. I didn't know whether I was coming or going half the time. For several months, I walked around in a semi-conscious state just from being tired and burnt out. I knew that I was acting irresponsibly, but I felt entirely justified in my behavior. I thought I deserved to have a good time and to let my hair down for once in my life. As always, I was searching for something to fill the emptiness I felt inside.

One night I came home late from a night on the town and was surprised to see Jim pulling in at the same time without Mallory. I inquired about her, and he informed me they were getting a divorce. I couldn't believe what I was hearing. I always felt they were the perfect couple.

We stood out front of our apartments talking for a while, and he continued to share his problems with me. He said Mallory had returned to her home state of Indiana because she didn't love him anymore. Jim seemed genuinely distraught, and my heart went out to him. In all honesty, I suppose I was a tiny bit excited and hopeful that I stood a chance with Jim now that Mallory was out of the picture. I couldn't believe she would leave a man like Jim when I would have given anything to be in her place. I was very attracted to Jim from the day I met him, but I kept it to myself.

Months passed, and summer was in full swing again. We were back to our usual routine of going to the pool every weekend. Jim always came down and joined us with a few beers in his cooler. I really enjoyed his company. He was very charming to me, and he was extremely good with Cliff. His manner was soft and playful with my baby, which made him even more desirable. I'm sure my flirtation was noticeable even though I tried to keep it subdued.

After a few weeks, Jim called me and asked me to go to a hockey game with him. I was thrilled he had called and took about five seconds to accept his invitation. We had a blast that night, and I was hopeful it wouldn't be the last. The atmosphere at the game was electric, and the players were extremely violent. So many fights broke out that the ice shavings were pink from the blood as they cleaned the ice. Jim drank his beer and screamed with excitement. The more violent the game got, the more he enjoyed it. I had never been to a hockey game before, but I really enjoyed myself. I hoped that this was the beginning of many more evenings with Jim.

The next day when I arrived home, there were flowers at my door with a note attached that read, "Thank you for a wonderful evening. How about dinner tonight?" It was signed by Jim. I was twenty-one, had been married and no one had ever given me flowers. I was very impressed that after only one date, he had sent me flowers.

That night we went out for a beautiful dinner at an expensive restaurant. As with the flowers, I had never experienced a romantic dinner in my life. McDonald's and hamburger joints had been the extent of my wining and dining up to this point in my life.

The next afternoon I came home to flowers again. I couldn't believe this was happening to me. For an entire week I saw Jim every night, and every afternoon there would be more flowers with a note attached. On the seventh day, the note read, "You are the most exciting girl I have ever known. I think I'm falling in love with you. I'll call you later. Jim."

I read the note and butterflies began to flutter in my stomach. The phone rang, and my palms began to sweat. I answered the phone and heard his voice on the other end. "Did you get my note?...Well, say something!" I didn't know what to say. I was smitten! No one had ever been so nice and attentive to me.

A few weeks passed, and I took Jim home to meet my mother, but I was surprised at her reaction. She was very cold and indifferent to him, and I couldn't understand why. It was funny, I thought, because Sandy had the same reaction. I began to feel like the people I loved the most didn't want me to be happy.

I decided to ignore their indifference and do as I pleased. It felt great being showered with affection, and I had no intention of giving it up. Jim was my knight in shining armor! I was going to play it to the hilt.

We dated regularly and were together most of the time. There were mornings I would leave for work and look up at Jim's apartment hoping to catch a glimpse of him. Many times he would have a big sign in his window for the entire world to see that read, "I love you, Dell." He wasn't afraid to show his feelings toward me, and I loved it. Well, it didn't get any better than this. He was handsome, he had a good job, he loved me, and he was great with Cliff. I was on cloud nine.

Sandy became involved in a relationship of her own, so we were both busy doing our own thing. She babysat when I went out, and when she went out, Jim and I took the baby with us or just hung out at the apartment. Jim was extremely possessive, but I found this appealing. It showed how much he cared for me, and I was flattered by the attention. I soaked it up like a sponge. I knew I wanted to spend the rest of my life with this man.

We dated for a year, and it was, without a doubt, the best year of my life at that point. On the eve of our one-year anniversary of dating, Jim took me out to a special romantic dinner. He ordered champagne, and at the end of the dinner, he got down on his knees in front of everyone and proposed. This was my dream come true. My ship had finally come in. My search for true happiness had come to a close, and I knew I had to be the happiest person in the world. The only thing I dreaded was telling Sandy and mom.

Soon afterward we were married by a Justice of the Peace. I had always wanted a church wedding, but church had become a thing of the past for me, and Jim certainly wasn't into it. It wasn't an ideal wedding, but that seemed relatively unimportant in the scheme of things. After all, I was marrying the man of my dreams.

Sandy (My sister from another mother)

Chapter 10

Captive

That night we drove Cliff to my mom's house so we could leave for our honeymoon. Jim knew how much I loved Florida, so he planned a romantic honeymoon in Miami Beach. I hadn't been to Florida since Sandy and I went to Daytona Beach several years before. I could hardly wait to spend a week with Jim in paradise.

When we finally reached our hotel, we were exhausted from the long trip. We grabbed a quick bite to eat and headed straight for our room. After soaking in a hot bubble bath for what seemed like an hour, I dressed in my new negligee. Jim was very sweet and tender, showering me with love and compliments. We climbed into bed, began to talk and he started asking me some very personal questions. He indicated that now that we were married, we had to be completely honest with each other, and I agreed. He continued by saying he had not been completely honest with me and wanted to set the record straight. My heart began to pound as I looked at him with tremendous anxiety wondering what I was about to hear. Jim proceeded to say I wasn't his second wife, but that I was his fourth wife. There had been two others I didn't know about. One wife had been killed in an automobile accident, and he had divorced another. Together with Mallory and me, he had been married four times! I couldn't believe what I was hearing. How could the man I had loved and trusted for more than a year keep from me something that important?

I was shocked and heartbroken. I began to sob uncontrollably, and suddenly, I noticed Jim's countenance changing. He didn't have the face of a man who was sorry for hurting me. He was clearly angry at my response, and I was totally confused by this. I was the one who deserved to be angry. How dare he treat me like this! I was crying uncontrollably, and suddenly he shouted, "Shut up, shut up, you ------! Do you hear me?" I couldn't believe my ears. Defensively, I muttered, "Jim, what's wrong with you? Why are you acting like this? Why are you ruining our wedding night? You're scaring me! Please stop."

Jim became even angrier and began asking me lurid questions about my past. "Well, my sweet, how many other guys have you been with?"

"What? No one but my ex-husband!" I explained.

"I don't believe you," he said with an almost demonic look on his face. "It's true! I've never been with another man," I stated emphatically.

He insisted, "I've been honest with you. If you really love me, you'll be honest with me."

Sheer terror began to well up inside me for I knew I was dealing with someone I didn't know. How could this be happening? I tried to change the subject, but he persisted in his interrogation. Suddenly, he jumped over the top of me with his fist balled up and demanded once more, "If you don't tell me the truth, I'll beat it out of you. Do you hear me, you bitch?"

"Oh, god!" I thought, "What have I done? Who is this man?"

I was shaking to the point that my body was convulsing with fear. Jim drew back his fist and hit me in the face so hard that I was dazed. Then, he hit me again and again and again. Was he going to stop or was he going to kill me? He hit me until he wore himself out, and then he collapsed on the bed in a fetal position crying like a baby.

My stomach was so upset that I vomited all over myself and there was blood gushing out of my nose and mouth. My ears were ringing, my head was spinning, and my vision blurred. I was sure he was going to kill me. My pain was so severe that I could barely move, and yet, I felt like I was having a bad dream. Needless to say, I was completely traumatized and terrified by what had happened.

All of a sudden, he crawled up close to me and cradled me in his arms sobbing out of control. He rocked me like a baby and asked me why I had made him hurt me. He said he loved me so much he couldn't bear the thought of ever having shared me with another man. I said nothing. I must have been in complete shock. I knew I wasn't dealing with a rational man, and I had no idea what I was going to do next.

As I lay there completely helpless, Jim violently raped me in my own blood and vomit. After he finished, he told me how much he loved me and not to worry because everything would be all right. How could anything ever be all right again?

I knew I had to get away from there that night. After he went to sleep, I grabbed my clothes and slipped out of the room. I was shaking so hard I could hardly walk. I was weak, terrified and badly hurt from the beating. I tried to hide my face when I walked through the lobby, but I was sure everyone saw me. I passed a mirror and caught a glimpse of the horrible looking creature he had made me. I nearly fainted when I saw the condition of my face.

How could I have been so stupid? Mom and Sandy were right! All of a sudden, I flashbacked to Mallory's black eyes, and it was all beginning to make sense for the first time. Why was I so blind? In my search to find true love, I had settled for a counterfeit. I realized for the first time that I had never really loved Jim, but I was in love with what he represented. I was in love with love itself, and it had blinded me to Jim's true nature. The warning signs were there, but I ignored them, and it had almost cost me my life.

There was no time to sit and reflect, I had to get out. I had to get out, but I had no money. I started off down the street walking and then running. Where was I going? I didn't know. I just had to get away and get away immediately. Suddenly, a car pulled up beside me. Oh no! It was Jim. He yelled, "Get in the car now!"

I tried to run, but there was nowhere to run, and I was afraid he might try to run over me. I got in the car, and he began yelling loudly, "Where were you going? Did you think you were going to leave me? How dare you walk out on me? I'll kill you before I see you with anyone else. I own you now, you ------."

He drove a few miles down the road and then pulled over and kicked me out of the car into a ditch and yelled out as he was leaving, "I'll read about you in the paper tomorrow you stupid slut."

I laid there in the ditch for a few moments feeling like I

had been left in an open grave to die. My life was in shambles, and I believed that I deserved it because of my poor choices. I wanted to cry out to God, but I thought I didn't deserve God's help because I was stupid and unworthy. I didn't understand that He sent His Son to save people with shattered lives just like me.

I started walking aimlessly down the road, not knowing where I was going or what I would do. There were no words to express the depth of my fear, and I felt like I wanted to die. How could I go home and face the humiliation of making such a mistake? Everyone tried to tell me, but I wouldn't listen. I couldn't go back to Jim. I realized I didn't even know this man I had married. How could I have been so stupid?

Here I was in a strange city, not knowing anyone and I didn't have a penny to my name. I walked and walked, sobbing until I thought my eyes would burst. What was I going to do? The pain was unbearable, both physically and emotionally. My heart was broken. There are no suitable words to articulate the depth of my despair as I walked down that road.

I'm not sure how far I walked when my new husband drove up again. This time I didn't run because I knew there was no use trying to get away. Actually, I hoped he would go ahead and kill me. My life was over anyway. Instead, he got out of the car and walked over to me and gently picked me up in his arms like a baby. He carried me to the car, but I remained silent, afraid to set him off again. He was like Dr. Jekyll and Mr. Hyde. He had switched back-and-forth from demon to angel with a simple blink of an eye.

We drove back to the hotel, and he began to clean me

up. I never spoke a word. I laid there in a catatonic state frightened, confused and crushed emotionally. Then, just as suddenly as he had changed into a monster, he again became the Jim I had loved, tenderly caressing me all night, apologizing relentlessly. I wondered what kind of man this was that could be so brutal one minute and so tender the next. The next morning when I awoke, I went into the bathroom to see the extent of my injuries. My face was swollen, my eyes were black, and the whites of my eyes were red where blood had settled. My lips were split open, bruises covered my face, and my eyes were so swollen I could barely see.

Jim came into the bathroom, hugged me like nothing had happened, and asked what I wanted to do for the day. How could he be so nonchalant about everything? Did he really think I could forget everything that had happened on my wedding night?

I felt trapped. I wanted to go home, but something made me stay. The next few days were as good as could be expected under the circumstances. Jim tried to be kind and loving as one would expect a new husband to be, but nothing could ever be the same. After we returned home, I made excuses to stay away from everyone until my face was back to normal. After I was finally well enough that people wouldn't be suspicious, I came out of hiding. I told everyone we had a wonderful honeymoon. I was too embarrassed to tell the truth. I wanted to believe this had been an isolated incident and things would get back to the way they had been before we were married. I rationalized that I had done something wrong to provoke him into such a rage. I just couldn't cope with being alone again and facing all my friends with the fact that I had made another mistake.

Months passed, and things were going pretty well. There had been no further abuse, so I felt maybe everything might work out after all. Jim became increasingly more possessive; however, I knew better than to complain. It got to the point where he wouldn't let me leave the house without him. He wanted to maintain total control, refused to give me any money and didn't want me to work. That didn't bother me too much because I loved being home with Cliff.

Approximately six months had passed, and I grew unhappier by the day. I realized I had become a slave to this man with no life of my own. All I did was cater to his every whim in fear he would snap at any moment.

One day I cooked a really delicious meal. It was Jim's favorite dinner of pot roast, mashed potatoes and vegetables. He came in from work and seemed a little stressed out, but I didn't question him. I encouraged him to sit down and relax while I brought him his dinner. Jim enjoyed bread with his meals, and I always tried to accommodate by preparing homemade bread every day. I had run out of ingredients to make the kind of bread he liked, so I substituted by placing a slice of white bread on his plate. I handed him the tray and sat down on the sofa beside him. Fortunately, Cliff was in his crib asleep.

I looked at Jim, and suddenly his entire face began to change, just as it did on our wedding night. His countenance changed to that of a crazed person. He threw the plate of food at me in outrage and said, "How dare you prepare me a wonderful meal like this and serve light bread with it? I'll teach you." Using every expletive I have ever heard, he cut me into a thousand pieces and smeared food all over my face and hair. I cried and pleaded for mercy. "Jim, please don't hurt me. I'm sorry. It will never happen again, I swear. Please, please."

He just laughed and picked me up and threw me across the room with super-human strength. I flipped backward over an ottoman, hitting the floor so hard that my head snapped back. He then jumped on me and began pummeling me again. He struck so hard with one blow that I blacked out. The next thing I remembered was lying in bed naked and looking over at him lying beside me, naked as well. I can only speculate that he raped me while I was unconscious. My condition was deplorable. I tried to get up, but I couldn't move. I knew I was badly hurt and had to get to a hospital. I begged Jim to take me to the emergency room, but he refused. I'm sure he was concerned about repercussions for himself. I finally convinced him, but only after I swore to lie about what had happened. He said he would kill me if I told the truth, so I made up a big story that no one believed anyway.

The hospital admitted me and the nurse called my mother to come to the hospital. When mom walked into my room and saw me she nearly fainted. My own mother didn't recognize me. My face looked like it had been run through a meat grinder. My nose was broken, my brow bone was fractured, and I had concussions in both eyeballs. The doctors were concerned that I might lose sight in my left eye.

Mom was unaware of the first beating, and I had managed to put on a good act, but she was no fool. She didn't buy my lies at all. She confronted me with the fact that she thought Jim had beaten me, and I denied it. She threatened to kill him with her bare hands if she saw him again. She begged me to go home with her, but I told her I could handle my own life and refused her help. I just could not face admitting defeat. I didn't want anyone to know what a fool I had been, and in my pain, I couldn't stand the thought of mother saying, "I told you so."

I stayed in the hospital for about a week while I was recovering and day after day analyzed my life and the situation I had created for myself. My plan to capture Jim had been successful, but ultimately, I was the one who had become captive.

He called the hospital every day to check on me, and every phone call was syrupy sweet. Apologies were relayed with every breath. He pleaded for forgiveness and promised he'd never hurt me again. I was depressed and confused by all that had happened, but I felt like I had made my bed, and now I had to sleep in it no matter what the consequences were.

I know how stupid it sounds to say I went back to Jim again, but that's precisely what I did. Initially, there was a period of calmness, but it was soon followed by another violent outburst. The abuse began to get more and more frequent until it reached a point that I was getting a beating every few days. He became increasingly more perverted as well. I was definitely living with a psychotic man who was capable of most anything. He also became more creative with his abuse. Sometimes he would lock me in the closet all day when I had been a bad girl, or he would taunt me with a knife, twirling it in his hands as he looked at me with the eyes of a madman. He would beat me so often that my eyes were almost always black. He sarcastically called me his little badger-eyed bitch.

There was a multitude of thoughts running through my head. I hated Jim and my deplorable living conditions, but there were many things to consider. He threatened to kill me if I left him, and I knew he was capable of carrying out his threats. I didn't know what to do, but I was tired of living on the edge.

Finally, I had enough, and I had him arrested. He stayed in jail two days and posted bail. I swore out a peace warrant and went back home. I thought he was smart enough not to try to hurt me again because he knew he would go back to jail. Well, I was wrong once again. The peace warrant meant nothing to him. He only laughed at me and beat me even worse for having him arrested.

By now, he began to cover himself by hitting me in places where it wasn't as noticeable. He pulled my hair until large chunks would fall out and kick me in the groin, stomach, and head. Sometimes he would hit me in the head with his fist creating big knots all over my head. I would go days without brushing my hair because I couldn't stand to put a brush in my hair. He broke the cartilage in my ear in one manic occasion.

I tried to analyze what could make a man act in such a way, but nothing made sense to me. He came from a divorced family, but his mother seemed normal. He had spent a year in Vietnam. Maybe that had an impact on him. I came to the conclusion that he was a Ted Bundy type. Jim could be so charming, luring his women into submission, only to become a torrid, violent maniac who received physical pleasure from someone else's pain. I knew Mallory had been a victim, and I wondered about his other two wives. I became suspicious about the circumstances surrounding his second wife's death and decided that I would have to do something drastic before I became just another statistic.

Almost a year had passed since my nightmare had begun. As I sat on my front doorstep one warm summer day reflecting on the past year, and the words of my father cut through me like a knife, "Living makes dying look easy." Ironically, I now understood what he meant.

For weeks I lay in bed at night and prayed that Jim would be killed on his way home. I lived in constant fear of an impending catastrophe. I began to have nightmares of killing him in bizarre ways, and I realized that I had become as sick as he was.

I came to the conclusion that since God wouldn't kill him, the responsibility rested on my shoulders. I kept thinking of Cliff, now almost 3 years old, and what his future held. Although Jim had never hurt Cliff, I knew he was unpredictable, and I did not want to take any more chances. I knew it was only a matter of time before Jim would fly on a rampage, and it wouldn't stop until he killed me. I had visions of Cliff witnessing my murder and the lasting effects it would have on his life.

My plan was simple. I would wait until I was covered with bruises and then make my move to end my misery. I would then turn myself into the police when it was over and swear I had killed Jim in self-defense.

I considered buying a gun but quickly discredited that idea in fear he might find it first. I didn't have the stomach to use a knife, so I discarded that idea as well. Considering my options made me ill. I felt no love, only hatred and contempt mixed with a certain amount of pity. It was the kind of pity you feel for a wounded animal. Knowing if I got too close, this animal would bite, I carefully planned my strategy to put this animal out of his misery and out of mine as well. When the time came, I would know what to do. Little did I realize that day would come sooner than I had imagined.

Chapter 11

Happy Anniversary

It was June 17, the day of our one-year anniversary, a day designed for celebration, but the only reason I had to celebrate was that I had managed to survive a full year in hell.

I bought a new dress for the occasion, the first article of clothing I had purchased since our wedding. I had lost so much weight that none of my other clothes fit me. The dress was very simple and inexpensive, a navy-blue tailored dress with a V-neckline that showed just a hint of cleavage. It was very tasteful and unpretentious, but having something new to wear helped to lift my spirits.

Jim promised to take me out to a nice dinner, and I was looking forward to a night out away from the house that had become my prison. I bathed Cliff early and made arrangements for him to stay next door with a neighbor while we went out.

Jim came home early to prepare for an evening out. I was in the bedroom applying the finishing touches to my makeup when he walked in the door. I greeted him with a smile and said, "Happy Anniversary." He said nothing and just stood there staring at me. I could tell by the look on his face that I was in trouble. This look had become all too familiar.

Nervously, I asked, "How do you like my new dress? I wanted to look my best for you tonight. I hope you like it." He walked over to me, ran his fingers down the neckline of my dress and stared at my breast with a demented gaze that penetrated me like a knife. Then he reached up and with his thumb, smeared my lipstick across my face. Tears involuntarily ran down my face, and I started to tremble.

He wrapped his fingers around my throat and then in almost a whisper, calmly asked, "Who are you trying to look sexy for? Has your boyfriend been here today?"

Shivering, I said, "Jim, don't be silly, you know I don't have a boyfriend. I bought it for you. You're the only man in my life."

"You're lying. Do you think I'm a fool? Who have you been with?"

He then ripped the dress completely off my body and shoved me onto the bed. As he started toward me, I kicked him in the groin, and he dropped to his knees. I instantly knew I had signed my death warrant.

I frantically jumped up and ran into the living room. Jim followed screaming profanities at the top of his lungs. He leaped over the coffee table, tackled me to the floor, turned me over and straddled me with his knees. He slugged me in the face and stomach, again and again, leaving me dazed. Then he wrapped both hands around my throat, gritted his teeth and snarled. "I'll kill you this time, you --------."

His fingers squeezed tighter and tighter as I gasped for air. My heart was pounding, and I felt like my lungs would explode. I tried to loosen his grasp, but I didn't have the strength. I closed my eyes and slipped into blackness. I don't know how long I was out until my eyes opened, and I gasped for air. I felt the breath of life flow back into my body. I slowly sat up and looked around the room. Jim was sitting at the kitchen table drinking a beer and crying.

He heard me moving around and came to my side. "Thank God," he said. "I thought I had lost you. I'll never hurt you again, I swear. Please forgive me. When I saw you in that dress, looking so beautiful, I went crazy with jealousy. I love you so much. Why do you make me do these things?"

Jim helped me to the sofa and brought me a wet cloth to wash the blood from my face. He took me in his arms and whispered, "Happy Anniversary, baby," and he then took a shower and went to bed. Happy Anniversary? Happy Anniversary, indeed, I thought sarcastically.

I called the babysitter and told her I wasn't feeling well and asked if she would bring Cliff home for me. She walked over about 15 minutes later. I opened the door, and she took one look at me and gasped. Her mouth flew open, and she was about to speak when I put my finger to her lips and whispered, "Please, don't ask." I thanked her for her help and told her I would explain later.

Cliff was peacefully sleeping as I carried him to his crib. I stood there watching my little angel as he slept. I leaned over, kissed his eyelids and whispered, "I love you so much." I left his room and walked into the den. I pulled open the drawer of the lampstand and pulled out an old dusty Bible. I opened the pages and began to read, hoping to find an answer to my dilemma, but the words all ran together. I closed the book and began to pray, "Dear Lord, I can't take any more abuse. Forgive me for what I'm about to do. I'm sorry for being such a disappointment. I only ask that you take care of my baby. I love him so much. He deserves a better life. Keep him safe and help him to grow up to be a good boy. I am so sorry."

I calmly and deliberately walked into our bedroom, picked up a large, jagged rock used as a doorstop and walked over to Jim's bedside. He was sleeping on his back with his face exposed, unaware of his impending doom. In a trance-like state, I lifted the rock high above my head. In that brief moment, as a battle between good and evil waged inside of me, Cliff suddenly cried out, "Mommy, Mommy." The sound of his voice snapped me back to reality. Realizing Jim was beginning to stir, I hurriedly put the rock down before he had a chance to see what I was doing. As the tears flowed down my face, I crawled into bed, shaking with the reality that I could be capable of murder. At the moment, it had seemed to be the only answer to escape my pit of abuse and hopelessness, but had God heard my desperate prayer and intervened through the cry of my son? As I look back, I'm confident He did intervene, and He kept me from making the biggest mistake of my life.

The days following one of these episodes always left me feeling drained and physically ill, but I looked forward to the calm after the storm. Usually, Jim would be on his best behavior for several days afterward.

A couple of days later I woke up with a high fever and severe stomach pain. My symptoms were flu-like in nature but much more severe. I began vomiting violently and lost control of my bowels. The pain was so severe I couldn't walk or even straighten up. Jim came in and found me crumpled up on the bathroom floor covered with body excrement. I was crying with pain. I told him I had never been this sick, and I felt I needed medical attention. He helped me to bed and said, "You just have a case of the flu. You don't need a doctor. I have what you need." He put a pillow over my face so no one could hear my screams. I had no control over any bodily functions, but he didn't care, and the more distasteful my condition was, the more excited he became. He had reduced me to the lowest form of an insect, and in that, I was depleted of all self-respect and will to live.

Fortunately, Jim's mom came by for a rare visit that day. When she saw my condition, she immediately knew I needed medical attention. She told Jim she would take care of Cliff while he took me to the hospital.

Upon arriving at the hospital emergency room, the doctors carefully examined me and could not determine the source of my illness. They knew, however, that my condition was severe and opted to perform emergency exploratory surgery immediately. Upon opening my abdomen, they determined that I had peritonitis, better known as blood poisoning. One of my ovaries had ruptured as a result of damage from continuous beatings.

When I became coherent after the surgery, my physician came in to talk to me. He said I was a very lucky young lady. The blood poisoning had already entered my bloodstream, and I was only minutes away from perishing. If the poison had reached my heart, I would've died within a few minutes. What a paradox, the physician had considered me lucky, but I felt cheated.

Something inside me began to stir, almost as if there was something or someone else in control of my destiny. I wanted desperately to understand the feelings I was having. I knew for sure there was a better life, but I didn't have a clue on how to obtain it.

Two weeks in the hospital gave me a much needed rest and a sense of peace for a short time. I missed my baby, but I knew he was in good hands. My recovery period gave me a chance to try to clear my head and try to make some plans.

Jim came to see me one night while I was confined to the hospital. He hadn't been there very long when a nurse came in and told me I had to get out of bed and try to walk. The last thing I wanted to do was walk. I was so sore from the surgery that I felt my insides would spill out on the floor if I moved, much less stand to my feet. I could see there was no getting around it, so I cautiously and slowly stood up and began to shuffle down the corridor. I was still hooked up to an IV and drug it along beside me.

Jim was keeping me company as I walked. He said he had something he had to tell me. He said he was interested in another woman. I can't remember exactly how I responded, but I know I was relieved inside. I hoped this was my chance for freedom.

He looked at me with a puzzled look on his face, and said, "You don't care, do you? You don't love me at all. You're just playing some kind of game." He continued, "I was lying. I don't have a girlfriend; I just wanted to see if you really loved me." The next thing I knew I was on the floor. Jim had knocked me down and then ran down the hall like a coward.

One of the nurses saw what happened and banned him from the hospital. She befriended me, and I felt like I could confide in her. She told me I should get out as soon as possible and asked if I had any friends. I told her about Sandy but that I was too ashamed and embarrassed to call her. She encouraged me to try, and I said I would have to think about it.

I dreaded being discharged from the hospital. It had been a place of solace for me.

The day I left, the nurse who had been so kind to me rolled me down to be picked up. Jim was there in rare form as a loving husband. The nurse shot daggers from her eyes at him and turned to me and said, "Honey, don't forget what I said." I said my goodbyes and got into the car.

Chapter 12

Stalked/Naked and Afraid

I walked on eggshells for the next few weeks because I was afraid something would set Jim off and he would re-injure me where I had surgery. During my rehabilitation process, there was little I could do, so I used the time to plan my escape. Fortunately, Jim was on his best behavior, but I knew he wouldn't be able to control himself for much longer. Nearly losing my life had opened my eyes to the reality that I had to get away from Jim. Although he had threatened to find me and kill me if I tried to leave, I knew I would surely die if I stayed. Finally, I built up the courage, swallowed my pride and called Sandy in Atlanta.

It was wonderful to talk to my best friend again. We picked up where we left off, and I opened up and told her everything. She immediately insisted that I move to Atlanta so she could help me and Cliff get a new start. I would have saved myself so much pain and heartache if I had only swallowed my pride that first night in Miami and called Sandy.

There was no way I could let Jim know my plans, so I had to wait cautiously for the right moment to get out. There was too much danger in trying to leave while he was working because I was terrified he might show up while I was packing. Finally, the opportunity I had been looking for came to fruition. Jim was invited to go on a fishing trip over a weekend with some of his friends from work. The day he left, I kissed him goodbye and hoped it would be the last time I would ever need to pretend I cared for the man I so desperately despised.

I called Sandy, and she and a friend came and helped me load all my furniture in a rental truck, and we made a midnight move to Atlanta. I was free at last! I left no message, no forwarding address and no trace of my whereabouts. If he knew I was in Atlanta, he would track me down, no matter what he had to do. Cliff and I moved in with Sandy, and we were a threesome again.

It's hard to believe Jim had never hurt Cliff, but he always had been very protective of him and in fact, appeared to love him. Jim's problem was with women. He was a coward when it came to picking on someone his own size, so he took his anger out on women. I am so thankful that God protected Cliff from Jim's brutality. Cliff was only a toddler during that time and today has no memory of Jim whatsoever. For that, I am eternally grateful.

I found a good job very quickly. Even though I didn't have a high school diploma, I had the gift of gab and could easily convince employers that I would make a valuable contribution to the company. I had become a pro at masking my poor self-image. It was a matter of life and death, and I learned to do whatever necessary to survive.

Sandy lived in a one-bedroom apartment, so there wasn't room enough for Cliff and me to stay for an extended period of time. Sandy, as always, was wonderful and helped me get started with a new life. I rented an apartment close to my job and was doing pretty well. I had found a new sense of freedom, and I wanted to pick up the pieces of my shattered life, not only for my sake but also for Cliff's. I worked really hard and began to excel in my job.

I enrolled Cliff in a Christian daycare program, and he was adjusting very well. My life was definitely taking a turn for the better. I began to make new friends through Sandy, and with their help, I tried to forget the nightmare I had lived through. Two nice young men that lived behind me in the apartment complex were helpful when I needed any help with my car and, really, helped with anything else I needed.

A short time after I moved to Atlanta, Grib decided to join us. It was great having all of us together again. Grib even struck up a romance with one of the guys that lived behind me, and we all became the greatest of friends.

Months had passed, but I knew it would take years for me to regain my self-worth. Jim had left me a defeated shadow of my former self. I knew I didn't want to risk making another mistake and resigned myself to living alone with Cliff for the rest of my life. I had become bitter and depressed over what had happened to me, but I didn't know how to pull out of my depression. I hoped sleep would be a means of escape, but even sleep became my enemy. The dreams I had once enjoyed were replaced with vivid nightmares and flashbacks of the hell I had experienced. Fear was my constant companion, and night terrors awakened me night after night. There were many times that I bolted out of bed screaming, wet with perspiration from reliving my horror. Morning would come, and I would try to reassure myself I was free from Jim and knew I had to force myself somehow to forget.

One morning, after an exceptionally restless night, I realized I had overslept and jumped out of bed. Panicked, I hurriedly dressed, grabbed my car keys and ran out the door for work. As I approached the car, I smelled a foul odor that became stronger and stronger. I noticed the car door was ajar and felt nervous about moving closer. I rehearsed the previous night in my mind, and I knew I had locked the door. My heart began to race. As I opened the door, the odor engulfed me. In total shock and disbelief, I grabbed my face and screamed at the horrible sight. In the front seat of my car lay a mutilated dog with a note beside it saying, "You're next, baby."

"Oh God, he's found me, but how?" I cried. "I left no trace. This can't be happening!" I began to look around, terrified he was watching me. Hearing my screams, neighbors started to come outside. Unaware of what I had seen and the horror I was experiencing, they must have thought I was crazy.

One of the guys that lived behind me heard all the commotion and came to see what was happening. He tried to comfort me, but it was hopeless. He took control of the situation and told me to go inside while he cleaned out the car, and I went in and called the police. My friends vowed they would protect me.

The police were as frustrating as ever with their advice. They suggested a peace bond, but I knew how ineffective that had been in the past. I didn't know what to do. I couldn't keep running for the rest of my life. I felt so frightened and bewildered at that moment that I was sorry I hadn't killed him when I had the chance. I couldn't believe he had found me. I kept repeating over and over again, "What am I going to do? What am I going to do?"

I knew I would never be safe again. Jim was out there somewhere stalking me like a lion after his prey. He had sworn he would kill me if I ever left him, and now he knew where I lived. I couldn't help questioning, "Why me? Why was this happening to me?" I was only twenty-two years old, and already my life was filled with so much tragedy. Was there no end to my suffering?

I stayed the next several nights with friends. My mom called and said she wanted to see Cliff for a couple of weeks and asked if she could come pick him up. She drove to Atlanta to get him. I was relieved to know he would be safe until I could remove Jim from my life.

Somehow Jim was able to get my phone number and began calling me with vulgar conversation and threats of killing me. I had my phone number changed, but how long could I alter my life to avoid him? There were times he would follow me in the car, taunting me by driving along beside me or bumping the rear of my car as I drove down the highway.

One night he cornered me in the parking lot of a grocery store and rammed the side of my car over and over again. Terrified, I tried to get away, but I was trembling so hard I couldn't get my car in gear. After he played with my emotions, he would always stop for a while. He acted like a cat toying with its prey just before he went in for the kill. I remember seeing my cat batting around our hamster after it had escaped from its cage. It was as if the cat were saying, "Get up, run, I'm not through playing with you," but the poor little hamster was already dead. Metaphorically, Jim was the cat, and I was the hamster. I feared my time was coming too, but how and when? How long would he play with me before he came in for the kill?

I was so tired that my will to survive was deteriorating. I couldn't sleep, eat or think straight. I looked around every corner wondering when he would strike. I was careful to avoid being alone, but it wasn't always possible.

I came home late from work one night on one of those occasions where I found myself alone because I was unable to make arrangements with anyone. I sheepishly unlocked the door to my apartment and headed for the closest lamp. I made one step inside the door when I felt a hand go over my face and a cold blade at my throat. As he clutched me tightly in his arms, he whispered with a sinister voice, "Tonight you'll be mine completely, and then you'll die. I told you what I would do if you left me, but I guess you didn't believe me. You just sealed your fate."

I guess my will to live was stronger than I thought. I knew he planned to rape and murder me, so I had to think quickly. I had to outsmart him if there was any chance for me to survive. As he removed his hand from my mouth and turned me around, I smiled at him and asked him what took him so long. I told him how much I loved and missed him. I confessed I had made a terrible mistake by leaving him and that life wasn't worth living without him. I begged him to take me back as I began undressing in an attempt to seduce him. He was buying it. I could tell he was becoming vulnerable, and so I continued. He put the knife down and began undressing. I helped him. I felt disgusting and slimy, but my plan was working. It's amazing what measures a person is capable of stooping to when one's life is on the line.

I moved closer and whispered for him to go to the bedroom while I poured us a drink. I was very convincing, and he started walking in that direction. I went to the kitchen, took two glasses from the cupboard and ice from the freezer. I made my way to the back door, making as much noise as possible so he wouldn't get suspicious. I grabbed a throw off the back of the sofa and clanked the ice in the glasses as I nervously slid the chain off the back door latch. I knew it wasn't a flawless plan, but it was the only one I had. The chain was out. I opened the door and began running as fast as I could, barefooted and naked with only the throw covering my body. I ran and ran until I found an apartment with a light on. I pounded on the door yelling, "Help me, please help me." An older lady I had never seen before came to the door. I was embarrassed, humiliated and terrified out of my mind, but I was alive!

Chapter 13

The Stranger

Shocked and startled by my appearance and hysterical frame of mind, the lady invited me into her home. She shuffled me into her utility room while she quickly retrieved a robe from her closet to cover my nakedness. After hurriedly and nervously explaining my dilemma, we phoned the police. As usual, they came to the house and filed a report. After searching the apartment and finding no trace of Jim, they went on their way. They suggested that I stay with a friend for the rest of the night.

The lady who had been so kind to me offered to house me for the night. I am embarrassed to say, I cannot remember her name, but I will never forget her face. She had the face of an angel, with a spirit so sweet that she melted my heart.

We sat at her kitchen table until the wee hours of the morning, drinking coffee while I poured out my heart to her. The compassion in her eyes was warm and tender, and although she spoke not a word for hours, I knew she understood. After listening intently, she began to speak words of wisdom to me. She told me Jesus was the answer to my problems and my troubled soul. She read a few scriptures from the Bible and prayed with me. She held me in her arms, and as she wept tears of compassion, she proclaimed that Jesus loved me.

I think it was the first time anyone had ever actually witnessed to me in that way. I realized she had something I needed, but I rejected her invitation to accept Christ as my Savior. I suffered from tunnel vision thinking only of the acute seriousness of my own dilemma. Unless Jesus was willing to come down from heaven and physically eliminate Jim from the face of the earth, I didn't know how He could help me. I would never enjoy the peace she referred to until I was free of the threat of Jim. Although my mind was clouded by my fears, the seed was planted that night. She pledged her continued prayerful support and challenged me to seek Jesus with all my heart. She asked the Lord to reveal himself to me in a very real way. Later that night, in almost an act of defiance, I metaphorically shook my fist at God and challenged Him to reveal himself by ridding me of Jim.

Jim continued to taunt me for a few more weeks, but suddenly his harassment stopped. He seemed to disappear as mysteriously as he had appeared. I always wondered if my friends that lived behind me had anything to do with his disappearance. Being the coward that he was, I can only assume he wanted no part of tangling with someone his own size and moved back to Tennessee. In the back of my mind, I remembered the night I had challenged God and wondered if He had answered my prayer. I closed my eyes and breathed a quick, "Thank you," just in case.

Jim vanished from my life, but the scars he left would never leave. Yes, he was gone, but I was left emotionally bankrupt with my fears turning to phobias. There were many skeletons left in my closet, and my negative baggage was filled to overflowing. I was afraid of my own shadow and paranoid of anyone who came near me.

In an attempt to overcome my fear and poor self-esteem, I threw myself into my job. It was my only source for positive reinforcement, and I quickly learned that when I excelled, people would take notice and give me the attention I so desperately craved. I worked long hours and became recognized as one of the top three producers in my company. I worked for a small insurance company, and recognition was easily attainable for anyone willing to pay the price. My strong desire to succeed and become independent paid off, and I was promoted to district manager within a short time.

Seeking those strokes plunged me into becoming an overachiever and gave me the determination to be self-sufficient. Like Scarlet O'Hara in "Gone with the Wind," I vowed that I would symbolically never eat turnips again. I packed every hour with work, leaving no time to reflect. I wanted only to focus on the future. Thinking if I did not face the past, I would not have to deal with it, so I moved ahead. Trying to suppress my pain, I denied it existed. I became a comedian, masking my tears, and I grew pompous in an attempt to hide my insecurities. Everyone thought I was confident and charismatic, but under my charade of happiness and control was a pathetic, miserable woman who did the only thing she knew to survive. My emotions were unstable with my highs very high and my lows very low.

I boasted of needing no one, and yet I desperately needed to feel loved. The new challenges of my career were a band-aid covering my wounded spirit, but it could not cover up the immense void in my heart. In the natural, I had tried to fill the emptiness by various methods, but each one had failed me. And yet, when offered the real solution, Jesus

Christ, I rejected it.

In an attempt to soothe my increasing loneliness, I teamed up with a partner at work and found it to be a very successful technique. I was fortunate enough to team up with the regional manager's son, Dan. He was a bright young man who graduated from Georgia Tech. He had personality plus and a great sense of humor. We became good friends and made a great team.

After my divorce from Jim was finalized, Dan became a self-imposed cupid, trying to set me up with his friends. I was uninterested for obvious reasons. There was one friend in particular that he frequently mentioned named Cary. In my usual manner, I blew it off and told him to mind his own business.

Meanwhile, as I struggled to rise to the top, my young son was seriously overlooked. My own needs became paramount as I disregarded his needs. I thought I was being a good mother by providing for him, but in retrospect, now with a few more wrinkles and considerably more wisdom, I realize how self-absorbed I was. As a result of trying to lick my own wounds, Cliff was shortchanged. Those were the formative years of his life, but I was not there for him emotionally. Ironically, I was mirroring the behavior of my mom when my father died.

Chapter 14

The Athlete

One of my responsibilities as district manager was to maintain a full sales staff. This meant hiring and managing new agents. One night while I was out with friends, I met a guy who had recently come home from a tour in the Navy in Viet Nam. He had been discharged and was looking for work. Bill was a tall, handsome young man who I thought had a lot of potential as an agent. We met the next day to discuss the possibility of employment within our company. He was eager to prove himself, and I enthusiastically decided to give him a chance.

The next few weeks were filled with introducing Bill to the business and helping him secure his insurance license. We studied long hours at night and worked hard during the day. As fate would have it, Dan was promoted to the regional office, and therefore, I lost my partner. Coinciding with the loss of Dan leaving and Bill securing his license came the natural progression for Bill to become my new partner.

I must admit we became quite a team. As I mentioned earlier, Bill was extremely handsome and used his looks to our advantage. I used the skills I had developed to secure permission to enroll large businesses in payroll deduction plans. After setting up the enrollment, Bill would walk in with the applications in hand and the female employees would ask, "Where do I sign?" We had a valuable program to offer, but he sure had a way of making it look easy. We were making good money and enjoying every minute of it.

Bill was a talented athlete and was the star of a local Rugby Team. I went to several matches with him and was always amazed at the female groupies who fawned over him at the end of each match.

Bill was definitely a hunk in present day slang, but there was a deeper, more sensitive side to him. Working so closely with him made me realize, in actuality, he was as messed up emotionally as I was. He too had experienced a difficult childhood and was a product of a bitter divorce. To further complicate matters, at the age of fifteen, he had seen his younger brother killed in a tragic accident. Running from those memories, Bill gave up a college scholarship in track and joined the Navy. He became a member of the Navy Seal Team, one of the fiercest Special Forces teams in all the armed forces. The nightmare of his youth, coupled with the horror of what he saw in Viet Nam, had left him an emotional cripple.

The curtain now opened for Florence Nightingale to enter the stage. As I reached out to nurse his wounded spirit, I was unaware that my own Achilles heel was being massaged at the same time. Bill had a deep respect for my business savvy and became increasingly attached to my nurturing. My own insecurities were being relieved by the attention of such a sought-after macho guy. On the heels of two disastrous relationships, I felt my value as a woman had to be validated, so I was receptive to his attention.

As the months and seasons passed, we became inseparable. We were fortunate to win a trip to Acapulco in a sales contest, and it was there we discovered we shared an attraction for each other that went beyond friendship.

After we returned from our trip, Bill came over one night and admitted he was falling for me. I sloughed him off and told him he was only infatuated. Fearful of letting myself become vulnerable, I resisted his affections. We continued working together, trying to deny the growing passion we were experiencing. I had been taught it was unprofessional to get involved with a co-worker, so I made a conscious effort to remain just friends.

It became more and more challenging to keep our relationship status quo, but neither of us had a healthy perspective of what real love was all about. We only had fantasies to draw from because neither of us had ever experienced a lasting, loving relationship. A pattern had definitely been established. I gravitated toward unhealthy relationships because deep down inside I felt like I didn't deserve any better. In a sense, I subconsciously sought relationships that reaffirmed my notion that I was unworthy of true happiness.

Discouraged by my aloofness, Bill began to date other girls. One night he brought one of his dates over for me to meet. It was a very unusual night because it stirred feelings of jealousy in me that I was unprepared to handle. I realized I either cared more than I wanted to admit or it was the competitive nature in me rearing its ugly head.

After a couple of drinks and a few tense moments, Bill took his date home leaving me alone to sort out my confusion. Tired from the day's events, I decided to rest and drifted off to sleep. I had only been asleep for a short while when I was awakened suddenly by the doorbell. My heart began to pound because my initial thought was one of fear that Jim had resurfaced. As I cautiously walked to the door, I began my strategy.

"Who is it," I nervously questioned. I heard Bill say, "It's me, Dell, please let me in. I need to talk to you." Relieved it was Bill, I unlatched the door. He came in and sat down on the sofa and motioned for me to join him. As he struggled for the right words, he lowered his head and said, "I love you, Dell." I can't go on pretending we're only friends. It's killing me, we belong together, and you can't deny it."

What should I do now? I was afraid to love again but also afraid not to give it one more chance. Surrendering my will, I decided to try once more with an attitude of what's one more mistake. I knew Bill aroused feelings in me, but I could not distinguish their true nature. Physical attraction was definitely a factor but certainly not enough to be the foundation for a relationship. I liked Bill an awful lot, but I wasn't sure I loved him. I did know that he made me feel alive. I reasoned with myself that I had married twice for love but was unsuccessful both times. I was determined never to allow myself to be hurt again. There were no delusions in the relationship. Being less than head over heels in love provided a safety net for being hurt again.

Bill and I began feverishly working on another sales contest. This time it was a week in Madrid, Spain, and we had six months to qualify. As our relationship progressed and the award seemed imminent, we planned our wedding to coincide so we could spend our honeymoon in Spain. We worked hard during the week and played hard on weekends. Soon our dreams were realized, and we qualified for our trip.

We said our marriage vows before a justice of the peace and were on our way to Europe.

After spending an adventurous honeymoon in Spain full of fun and passion, we headed back to Atlanta to plan our future together as husband and wife. Bill took advantage of his entitled military benefits, and we were able to buy a house in the suburbs. It was my dream house -- cozy and warm with a huge yard for Cliff to run and play. It was the first house for both of us, and we were so proud of it. Being a good wife, mother and homemaker was my number one priority. After all, I was in my early twenties and was already on my third husband. I had to make this marriage work for Cliff's sake as well as my own. Another failure was out of the question. In my heart, I felt I could not survive if this marriage failed. My fear of failure commanded me to strive to make Bill happy no matter what the cost, and I catered to his every need.

Meanwhile, our business was thriving. We continued to work together on a daily basis. Our weekends were occupied with rugby games and having fun with Cliff. We bought two Samoyed puppies for Cliff and a sports car for ourselves. We were quite a family, and I was the envy of every rugby groupie in Atlanta.

After one of the rugby matches, a representative of a modeling agency approached my husband and told him he had great potential. They booked an appointment, and within a few weeks, they put together a stunning portfolio for him. We were both very excited and very flattered, but all the attention he received created tremendous anxiety in me and magnified my existing insecurities.

As the months passed, our lives blended into the first

normalcy I had ever experienced. Although I was happy and our future looked bright, I knew there was still a void in my life that I couldn't deny. On the surface I had everything, but all the trauma and failures of my past had left me without peace deep down inside. Everything I was experiencing with Bill felt superficial, and after the newness wore off, I began to settle into a deep depression and a feeling of extreme emptiness.

One day as I was in the yard playing with Cliff, my neighbor came over to chat. Bill was working out at the gym. I was nursing a toothache and having a real pity party. My neighbor was a good ole boy that was, in my opinion, a little over the top in his religious beliefs. He befriended us and tried to share his religious convictions with us. Bill was unreceptive to his witnessing, but I was curious. As we talked that afternoon, he eagerly shared the gospel with me. He was a bit on the redneck side with a country accent, and I must admit it was hard to take him seriously. However, it was his passion and sincerity that drew me. He spoke with love, and I knew his convictions were sincere. As we continued to talk, my toothache intensified, and then he dropped a bomb on me. He invited me to attend a church that night to hear an evangelist who was known for his teeth healing ministry. Laughing hysterically, I told him he was crazy.

Bill came home, and I extended the invitation for him to join me. He emphatically declined, but the pain in my tooth, coupled with extreme curiosity compelled me to go. At least I thought that was the reason that I felt compelled to go.

I arrived late to the small church in Smyrna, Georgia, nervously entered and sat on the back row with the service well under way. What I witnessed startled me because I had never seen anything so strange. The evangelist placed his hands on people as they came forward and prayed for healing for their teeth problems. As he prayed, they fell to the floor, and I heard them speak a language that was foreign to me. To say I was freaked out is an understatement. One woman had a mirror and held it to her mouth. She yelled out, "Look, I have a new tooth." People were crying and laughing as they lay on the floor. Some received gold crowns. I was intrigued but too scared to ask for prayer, so I went home with my toothache.

Anxiously, I hurried home to tell Bill what I had experienced and was awake all night thinking about my encounter. I begged Bill to go back with me on Sunday morning. In my mind, I thought if this was happening on a Wednesday night, what in the world would we see on Sunday.

I was restless over the next few days because my heart was stirred by what I had seen at church and by what I was feeling. I realized there was a giant hole in my heart that I had tried to fill with wrong behavior and relationships. My tears would not stop flowing. I pleaded with Bill to go with me on Sunday, and he finally, but reluctantly, agreed. He had a rugby match that afternoon, but he consented as long as we could leave early if the service ran late.

We sat on the back row and nervously anticipated what might happen. The evangelist was no longer at the church, but the pastor, Reverend Marty Tharp, approached the pulpit. As he spoke, the love he portrayed brought me to a place I had never experienced. His message revealed the unconditional love of Jesus Christ. As I held on to every word, the realization that I had never been loved unconditionally penetrated into my soul. Everything I had experienced had been counterfeit and based on my performance and success. As far back as my childhood, I had never known that type of unconditional love. My tears flowed soaking my clothes, and my body shook uncontrollably. As Pastor Marty gave an altar call, I felt like a giant magnet was pulling me to the altar, and I ran as fast as I could with no hesitation. All my inhibitions were canceled, and I no longer cared who was watching. Bill stayed seated, but his reluctance did not deter me.

That day my life was changed. I was born again, all my sins were washed away, and I knew I would never be the same. That morning the emptiness in my heart was filled with Jesus. I realized for the first time that the only one that could truly satisfy my heart was the One who created it. Everything in my life had brought me to this place at this time. I was emptied out at the altar and filled with a new joy and peace that I had never known. My search was over for I had found true love in my Savior Jesus Christ.

Chapter 15

Betrayed

After the service, Pastor Marty greeted us at the door. He asked us to join him and his family for lunch, but we declined as we had to get to the rugby match and we were already running late. Marty asked where the match would be held. At first, I thought he was simply making conversation but quickly realized he wanted to join us. Anxiety gripped us both. There was no way we could allow him to go to a rugby game and be subjected to the foul language, drugs and alcohol that accompanied every game. We nervously stated it was no place for a pastor, and surprisingly, he laughed. He said, "That sounds like the place I need to be." Oh my, there was no getting around it. Pastor Marty was determined to go….and he did. At one point the players were running around in only their jock straps. I was completely mortified and embarrassed, but Marty seemed unaffected by their vulgarity. Instead, he greeted each player with love and dignity. Despite my humiliation, I knew this man was sent by God to change our lives. He befriended us and showed so much love that it wasn't long before Bill gave his heart to Jesus also.

Our lives were changing rapidly. We jumped in with both feet and became very involved in the ministry. Marty was a Bible scholar and taught us so much. I held onto every word he spoke. I felt like Grasshopper in the TV series Kung Fu. Grasshopper was an understudy, and he would say, "Oh tell me, Master," as he gleaned from his mentor's wisdom. I was so eager and hungry to hear about the word of God.

Eagerly, I even joined the choir. If you ever heard me sing you would realize how devoted I was because I can't sing a note. I felt such peace around Marty and his wife Sharon that I wanted to spend every minute with them.

Finally, my life was complete. I had a good marriage, and I had found Jesus. Life was good. The hole in my heart had been filled, and I was genuinely happy for the first time in my life. I was overwhelmed with joy. Each day was a new adventure, and I grew each day spiritually. Life was going so well that Bill and I decided to expand our family. About six months later I was overjoyed to discover I was expecting a baby, and my heart was full to overflowing. Yes, everything was going my way for once in my life.

Bill's modeling career was growing, and so was my girth. As I began to manifest the usual symptoms of pregnancy, I noticed a change in Bill's attitude toward me. He seemed to be distancing himself from me. Concerned about his demeanor, I spoke to a close friend about the strain on our relationship. She reassured me that it was relatively common for men to become distant during their wife's pregnancy. I shrugged it off and realized I had to try harder in my marriage.

A few days later I was preparing Bill's favorite meal

when he called and said he would be late for dinner because he had an unexpected photo shoot. Disappointed, I told him I would keep his food warm for him. The more I thought about it, the more compelled I felt to drop by and take his dinner to him. After all, the photo shoots often lasted for hours. In my determination to be a good wife, I decided to go with my gut instinct.

As I arrived, I saw his car and one other car. The spa was closed so I naturally assumed the car belonged to the photographer. As I opened the back door, I heard laughter. Smiling, I entered the facility and walked quietly toward the sounds being careful not to disturb the shoot. Holding a plate of hot food, I tiptoed to the wet room. My heart sank. There was my husband with one of the exercise coaches locked in an embrace. They were so involved in their intimacy they did not realize I was watching them share their passion in the hot tub. Suddenly, Bill turned around, saw me and gasped as he hurriedly reached for a towel to cover himself. "I brought your dinner to you," I said, and then I threw the plate at him and ran out the door.

Where do I go? What do I do now? My life flashed before me as I left the haunting scene of my husband in the arms of another woman. My body convulsed and trembled as I threw up in the car from crying hysterically. This cannot be happening. Am I so unworthy to be loved? I must be a terrible person. Nobody loves me. I thought I found the missing peace in my life when I gave my life to the Lord. Oh God, where are you? Every male figure in my life had hurt and disappointed me starting with my own dad, now a third husband, and, yes, even my heavenly Father. My dreams were crushed once again, and at that moment, I resolved that I must be a wretched person, so bad that no one could love me. I wanted to die.

How could this be happening? Once again, I was alone, pregnant, facing a divorce and now I would have two small children to raise alone. I questioned everything in my life. Most of all I weighed my validity as a worthwhile human being. Distraught, scared and confused I headed to Marty's office. It was late, but Marty was still there studying. I stormed into his office and began to scream profanities at him. "You're a liar. Everything you led me to believe is a lie. Why? Why? You're supposed to have all the answers. I trusted you. What am I supposed to do now?"

Marty tried to console me, but I was in a state of uncontrollable rage and total despair. His words, though sincere, fell on deaf ears. I ran out of the church dazed and panicked, desperate to soothe my aching heart.

The only conclusion that made sense was the realization that I must be a loathsome person. Unconditional love was a fantasy. Therefore, I set out to validate my theory by acting the way I felt. Feeling undesirable I got dressed in the most seductive outfit I could find and went to a nightclub. Trying to drown my sorrows in alcohol, I drank heavily. A guy seeing my vulnerability made his move on me like a wild animal stalking his prey. In my intoxicated state and my wounded spirit, I succumbed to his flirtations. Leaving my car at the club, I went to his apartment with him. With seductive music, alcohol and an attitude of I don't care what happens, the stage was set for disaster, but as things began to heat up, we were interrupted by the phone ringing. My suitor answered the phone, and the puzzled look on his face was apparent. "What?" he said. "Who is this? Yes, just a minute," and handed me the phone. The look on my face had to be shocking. I nervously held the phone to my mouth and inquisitively said hello. Shocked, I heard a familiar voice. "Delbert, what are you doing?" Delbert was a pet name that Marty called me when he was frustrated. "Marty?" I asked puzzled. "How did you get this number?" He spoke with authority, "Get your little fannie over here right now," he demanded. "Now, Delbert, I mean it!"

How did he know where I was? Did he follow me? How did he get this guy's number? I had so many questions, but all I knew was that I had to get out of that apartment and get to Marty's place in a hurry.

I begged the guy to take me back to my car, but he declined. He had other things on his mind, but I knew I had to leave, so I ran out the door and called a taxi from a local pay phone. I picked up my car and headed to Marty's office. When I arrived, Marty was sitting in his easy chair reading his Bible. He looked out over the top of his glasses and directed me to sit down. I immediately started firing questions at him. How did you find me? Did you follow me? How did you get the phone number? Marty said he had been praying ever since I left his office. He knew I was self-destructive, and he prayed God would show him how to help me. He said that after hours spent in prayer, the Lord told him to pick up the phone and dial and He would give him the number. Clearly, God was trying to get my attention, but in my state of mind, I ignored the unmistakable hand of God working on my behalf. As a new believer, I had not yet experienced God's help and guidance in devastating moments like the one I had just suffered. This was the first of many miraculous events that I would experience under the shepherding of Reverend Marty Tharp.

The Royal Hotel Cookstown
Photographer Richard Mckeown

My spiritual parents,
Drs. Marty and Sharon Tharp

Chapter 16

Deceived

Run, Dell, run as fast as you can, I thought. The Lord was performing one miracle after another to show me His love and power, but my mind only said run. The Lord was speaking loud and clear, but I couldn't hear him because I was so broken and confused. Bill was gone, Cliff and I were alone, and I was pregnant. I trusted no one, and I hated everything and everybody who came near me. I stopped going to church and wallowed in my pain.

One night it was storming as I was driving home from work. When Cliff and I went inside our home, I discovered my power had been cut off. It was cold outside, and I had no electricity. As I sat down, I tried to hide my tears from Cliff when once again the phone rang. On the other end, I heard the familiar voice ask, "Delbert, what's wrong?" "Nothing Marty," I replied, "nothing." Marty continued, "Delbert, the Lord said you were in trouble, and the Lord doesn't lie." I cried harder. Who is this man, I thought, who hears from God like Moses did? He demanded that I go to the church immediately or he would come to my house. I didn't want him to see my power off, so I agreed. As I entered Marty's office, he said, "Hit 'em Delbert," which meant get on my knees. He began to ask God how he could help me. After praying, he got up, sat behind his desk, opened the drawer and pulled out an envelope full of money. He reached in the envelope and handed me the exact amount I needed to turn on my electricity. One would think this was enough to turn me around, but the depth of my anger and despair was over-powering everything and clouding my vision. God was right there, meeting my needs, but I couldn't see Him. Could I ever trust Him again?

On another occasion after leaving church, Marty looked at my car and noticed my tires were slick and needed replacing. I informed him that I had no money. Marty prayed and told me to get in his car. When we got into his car, I asked him where we were going. He said he had a friend who owned an auto salvage yard and we would find tires there. When we arrived at the yard, his friend greeted us, and Marty asked him if he had tires to fit my car on his lot. His friend looked at his inventory sheets and said that there were no tires that would work. Marty looked at him and said, "The Lord said there were four tires here and the Lord doesn't lie." The man laughed and said, "Well Marty, you're welcome to look around, but you won't find anything." Marty said, "What if I do?" His friend laughed again and said, "Marty, if you find tires that are the size you need, you can have them!" We started searching the lot and found nothing. Then we saw a shed way in the back of the lot and headed toward it. It was filled with so much junk we could barely get through it. Marty told me to wait for him. I heard Marty laughing and praising God, and then he walked out with two brand new tires still wrapped in paper. He looked at me and said,

"Delbert, there's two more in there just like it, and they are exactly the size you need. Trust God, Delbert, trust God because the Lord doesn't lie." This truth was going to be invaluable to me in the years to come.

Despite God's miraculous provisions, life was hard. I couldn't focus on work or being a good mom or anything productive. I called Bill and begged and pleaded for him to come back home. With all hope gone, I went to the home of his girlfriend and knocked on the door. Bill opened the door. He said "What are you doing here? What do you want? You shouldn't have come here." His girlfriend approached me and said that Bill didn't love me anymore and wanted to be with her. Like a groveling weakling, I told her I was pregnant. She told me not to worry. They had discussed the situation, and she was prepared to raise my baby. What? In a rage, I told her she would never touch my baby. I would make sure that would never happen! They said if I didn't leave they would call the police. At the moment, I hated them so much that I believe I could have killed them both. She had my husband. There was no way she would have my child!

I went to bed that night pondering my hopeless situation, depleted of all common sense and reasoning. I decided there was no way I could bring another child into my life. I didn't feel capable of raising another child because nothing was going right. Nothing. I couldn't work, I was broke, and I was crippled emotionally. What kind of mother could I be anyway? My children would have no hope of a happy life with me. I plotted and determined that I had to eliminate the problem by ending the pregnancy. I didn't consider seeking God's counsel in my situation because I was questioning everything I knew about Him. Instead, I listened to the lies of the enemy, Satan, who always seeks to destroy life.

The next day I went to a clinic and sought a solution. The doctor counseled me that he could perform the procedure, but since I was in my second trimester, twenty-four weeks, it could be complicated. The expense was enormous, and I didn't have the money, so I called my mom and asked her to give me the amount I needed. Knowing she wouldn't approve, I justified my decision with a lie. I told her I had a tubal pregnancy, and if I continued to carry the baby, it could be life-threatening. She cried but willingly sent me the money to save my life. I realized I could hide my shame by telling others the same wicked lie.

Two days later I checked into the hospital, and they wasted no time getting started. I was alone and afraid. The room was cold. In my naivety, I thought they would sedate me, I would wake up, and everything would be over, but that was only one more of the lies I believed. An expressionless nurse walked in with a very large needle. She offered no comfort and told me it was going to hurt. She plunged the needle into my uterus and extracted the amniotic fluid. Tears flowed from the pain, both physically and emotionally. As the fluid was drained, I felt my baby jumping and twitching. Oh God, what have I done? Oh God, I don't want to do this. But it was too late. What was started would end with giving birth to a lifeless baby. They injected saline into my uterus, and I began to throw up violently. Then the pains of child-birth threw my body into a convulsive state. It was the kind of pain that could only be forgotten by the joy of a baby's first cry, but that cry would never be heard.

For hours I lay there in excruciating pain that could only

be described as a feeling of my insides ripped out slowly and methodically until I gave birth. I screamed as I looked down to see I had given birth to a tiny baby girl. My screams alerted the nurse, and she came in and scooped up my little daughter and discarded her into a trash bin. She made no effort to console me but gave me morphine to ease my pain.

The reality of what I had done gripped me like a vice and wouldn't turn loose. I had taken the life of my own baby daughter. I could no longer justify my actions. Yes, I was weak and desperate, but it didn't excuse my choice. I looked in the mirror and was disgusted with who I saw, so disgusted that I climbed into the closet and huddled in the corner. I couldn't run from myself, I couldn't hide. I could only live with the decision I had made and the visual memory of what I had done.

Every day was a struggle. Sleep was my only escape, but the haunted visions I saw made sleep difficult. The demons in my head screamed deafening accusations: "You're no good, you deserve to die. You killed your own baby. No one loves you, you're unlovable. God will never forgive you." I cried out for God to make them stop, but the voices in my head were relentless.

There are no words to express the depth of my despair adequately. My whole life was one tragic event after another. I was paralyzed with gut-wrenching depression and guilt. The hole that swallowed me up was so deep, so dark that I reasoned only permanent sleep could rescue me from the pain. I felt Cliff would be better off without me.

In my despair, I went to my room and wrote a letter to be read to Cliff. My tears flowed in a steady stream. Then I called my mom and told her how much I loved her and

119

how sorry I was for all the mistakes I had made. We talked for a while and said goodnight. I walked to the bathroom, picked up a razor blade and sat on the side of my bed. I just wanted to sleep. I cried and screamed at God. Don't you care? Does anyone care? I put the razor blade next to my wrist and made a tiny slit. At that moment the phone rang. I reluctantly answered and on the other end of the phone was a pastor who had come to my church as a guest speaker. He and Marty were close friends. After he spoke at the church, they invited me to join them for lunch. It was a brief encounter, and I had not spoken to him again until this moment. He began the conversation by saying he was praying and the Lord showed him that I was in trouble and told him to call me. He called Marty, asked for my number and said to him that the Lord had given him a word for me.

When I answered the phone, he said, "Dell, This is Brother Johnson, and the Lord inspired me to call you because you are in trouble. He proceeded to tell me how much God loved me and how He had he collected every tear I had shed. He said, "The Lord said if I will walk the straight and narrow and lean on Him that He would bless me and give me back tenfold what the enemy had stolen from me." I cried so hard that I felt I would drown in my own tears. He talked and prayed with me until he was confident he had accomplished his mission from God. A spiritual war took place that night in my bedroom. Satan was already rejoicing, but the Lord intervened and won the victory and saved me from the snares of the enemy.

And then I slept!

Chapter 17

Seeing the Light

Weeks passed as I tried to gather the pieces of my broken life. I bought a condo for Cliff and me, and we hibernated in our new home. I was so full of shame that I didn't want to go to church. I was emotionally bankrupt and without hope. Besides, how could God forgive me for what I had done! What's more, I was angry with God for all my suffering and that I had lived such a painful life. If God loved me, why did my dad have to suffer and die, why did Rex leave me when I was pregnant with Cliff? Why did Jim beat me senseless? Why did Bill leave me for another woman when I was pregnant? I had so many unanswered questions. Once again my thoughts returned to the only plausible reason - it was my fault. I must be unlovable. I must be a horrible person. Yes, and now I had done the unthinkable in ending my baby's life.

Days turned into weeks and weeks turned into months. There was an aching in my heart, and there was a void that I now knew could only be filled by God. But how could I swallow my pride and have faith that He would even take me back? I continued in my day-to-day misery until I couldn't take it any longer. It had been many months since I had prayed. Oh, I often had screamed at God but had not actually talked to Him.

One night in my despair, I went to bed and began to talk to God for the first time in a long time. As I prayed His presence filled the room. His Holy Spirit was so thick I could no longer speak, and I lay for hours there as the light of His presence engulfed me. I could hear His still, soft voice saying, "I love you, I have been waiting for you." The next day was Sunday, and I could hardly wait to go to church and run to the altar. With a heart full of emotion, I had the confidence that God would meet me at the altar.

The alarm went off, and I walked into Cliff's room to awaken him for church. As he awoke from a deep sleep, I said, "Get up Cliff, we're going to church." He was so excited to go back to see Marty, Sharon and his friends in Sunday School.

We lived in Marietta, GA, and had to drive on the 285 Bypass to get to church in Smyrna. Our excitement was palpable as we approached the Smyrna exit. In the distance, I could see a huge transport truck crossing the bridge over the interstate. As I approached the intersection, I applied my brakes. To my horror, my brakes failed. All I could see was the truck barreling down on us. Realizing a collision was inevitable, I screamed, "Jesus, Jesus help me."

Instinctively, I grabbed Cliff and pulled him down in the seat and lay on top of him to secure and protect him as I locked my hands under the seat. And then the crash came, so violent that the car was catapulted into the air. The car flipped on its top and then back on its wheels over and over again until we finally came to a stop. The impact collapsed the roof on top of us entrapping us beneath the rubble. My attempt to cushion Cliff had saved me from being severed in half, but my body received the full force of the impact. Although I was severely injured, I was thankful that Cliff escaped unharmed. Several ribs on my left side were broken, piercing my lung, liver, stomach and spleen, and I also I had a traumatic brain injury. Cliff was screaming "Mommy, Mommy." His face was covered with my blood.

The truck driver was uninjured and quickly ran to our aid. He apparently was a man who knew the Lord because he called out to God as he frantically tried to rescue us. He cried, "What can I do? Oh God, help me." I asked him to get Cliff out of the car, and he managed to free him and lay him in the grass beside the road. I could still hear Cliff screaming my name. The truck driver came back to me and tried to free me from the wreckage, but I was trapped. The pain was unbearable. I asked him to knock me out. He said, "Oh God, ma'am I can't do that," but I pleaded. He wept as he prayed a gut-wrenching prayer for God to save me.

Within a few minutes, the fire department arrived along with the ambulance. I was slipping in and out of consciousness as they cut me out of the car. I heard them say, "We're losing her."

Meanwhile, a family that attended the church passed us and realized who we were. They took Cliff to the church and summoned the church to pray. Sharon took Cliff home with her and Marty met me in the ER where they were feverishly working to save my life. I was hemorrhaging to death from my internal injuries. My lungs had collapsed, and they were inserting breathing tubes into my lungs. In the midst of all this going on, I sensed my spirit hovering over my body as they worked on me. Surprisingly, I felt total peace. As

I watched them, I wondered why they were so worried and frantic. I overheard the doctor call my mom in Tennessee to tell her I was in critical condition and urged her to get on the next plane. I heard him say they were taking me into surgery and they would do everything they could to save me. Then I drifted back into my body. My nurse was wearing a cross. In my weakened condition, I asked her to pray, but the doctor responded there was no time to pray and that we had to hurry. Then I heard Marty say, "Praying may be the only thing we have time to do." He prayed as they were rolling me to the surgical ward. In my critical state, I cried out to God and begged for forgiveness vowing that if He saved me, I would spend the rest of my life serving Him. Marty held my hand until they rolled me into surgery. His last words to me were, "I love you, Delbert. God is with you."

When I awoke days later, I was on a ventilator and hooked up to all kinds of wires and tubes. When I was lucid enough to talk, I was told they almost lost me on the operating table. My heart stopped for several minutes. The defibrillator paddles were used as well as a shot of adrenaline to start my heart again. After many days in the hospital, they sent in a counselor to help me work through the psychological perspective of the trauma. I shared with her a supernatural experience I had experienced during surgery. She became very interested and documented my story.

I remember walking through a very cold, damp, dark tunnel. I was drawn to a bright light at the end of the tunnel. As I drew closer to the light, I could see a beautiful meadow full of vibrantly colored flowers. There was a crystal clear river that sparkled like diamonds. In the foreground was a large boulder with beams of light shining directly on the large rock.

It was the most beautiful, peaceful place I had ever seen. I reasoned that if I could cross over and lie against the rock, the heat from the light would warm me. Just as I prepared to step into the glorious place, I heard a voice at the dark end of the tunnel. I turned and saw Cliff standing there with his arms outstretched toward me crying, "Mommy, don't leave, please Mommy, come back." I answered back, "But Cliff, I have to leave." Again he cried, "I'm scared, Mommy, who will take care of me?" I answered, "Nanny will take care of you." Once again he cried, "No, Mommy, I love you. I want you. Please come back."

I was so torn. I wanted to go to this place of peace and warmth, but I could not leave my son. As I looked at him and then back to the light, I was torn with what to do. I turned toward my son, and that's the last thing I remember.

The counselor listened attentively. With tears in her eyes, she told me I had experienced a life after life phenomenon. She said others had shared similar experiences when they were on the brink of death. I now believe I was on my way to heaven when my heart stopped. The moment the defibrillator restarted my heart was the moment I decided to go back to my son.

Although I didn't make it to the church altar on that tragic day of the accident, God met me where I was. He spared my life and forgave me when I cried out to Him in my desperation.

Today my body is full of scars, but I have fully recovered. I love my scars because I look at them and I'm reminded that the Lord saved my son and me even though the enemy of my soul tried to end our lives. I knew my life would never be the same, and I had a promise to keep. Without a doubt,

God saved me for a reason, and I was on a quest to discover my destiny.

Chapter 18

Clueless

The weeks that followed the accident were difficult, to say the least. I was a mere shadow of my former self, weighing only ninety-eight pounds. My recovery was long and painful, but a friend volunteered to stay with me for a few weeks to help during my recovery.

As I progressed enough to drive, I eagerly headed back to church determined to live the rest of my life for God. Poor choices and emotional heartbreak had taken a toll on my son and me. Unfortunately, the choices I made were made out of fear, loneliness, and insecurity. I desired to make a better life for us, but in doing so, I failed to make the Lord my partner and the center of my life. I made choices out of desperation, and each poor choice made our lives more miserable. The choices we make in life not only impact our own lives, but they impact everyone we love as well. There is a reward or consequence for every choice we make. What I now understand is that without the Lord at the helm of our ship, we risk sailing into deep, murky water and stormy seas. Living for God doesn't mean we won't have troubles or encounter storms in our lives. However, if we trust in God and have faith, we are assured that He will guide us safely through the storm.

When I was a child, the suffering my dad endured left him unable to be the provider and Godly role model that I needed. He was strict and very tough on me. I was punished if I wasn't the best at everything I did. I pictured God was ready to punish me at any given time I didn't meet or exceed His expectations. Therefore, I had an unhealthy perspective of my relationship with my heavenly Father. Even Dad's early death at thirty-seven years old left me with a fear of abandonment, but thankfully I have learned that the Lord says, "Be strong and courageous. Do not be afraid or terrified because of them, for the LORD your God goes with you; he will never leave you nor forsake you." (Deut. 31:6)

Clearly, I needed a lot of healing emotionally and physically to take place in my life. Pursuing my healing would be a process for me. There are times God performs miracles, and our healing is instantaneous, but more often it takes time. I realize now that delay does not mean denial.

Because my life had careened entirely out of control, I questioned in my heart if I could ever attain wholeness. My dreams of a happy family life seemed unreachable. Oh, I still dreamed of a loving husband but felt unworthy to be loved and happy. Who would want someone who had failed in marriage three times? Therefore, I reasoned Cliff and I would be alone forever. I would seek God with all my heart and follow hard after Him, and I would put my energy into making the best life for us that I could. A romantic relationship was last on my list. Even though my dream was to be married, my self-esteem was at rock bottom, and I gave up on the idea.

Marty and Sharon were always there for me. My finances

had suffered from being out of work for so long. There were times I couldn't afford gas to get to work, but often, Marty would fill up my car with gas. Marty and Sharon were truly my spiritual mom and dad who literally loved me into the kingdom. God supplied my needs at every turn. Miracles were common in their ministry, and I grew in the Lord daily. I was finally learning to trust God. Marty spent hours explaining the ways of God and teaching me His Word. I thank God for the influence of these surrogate parents for Cliff and me.

Life was settling down, and Cliff and I were in a routine that was working for us. It's amazing how that can happen when your priorities are in line with God's Word. We didn't have much of a social life, but we were satisfied. I missed my best friend, Sandy, so much. She had moved to Florida, and we didn't have too much contact. Oh, how I missed her.

I had a few casual friends, but all were superficial compared to Sandy. My business partner, Dan, tried to set me up with an old friend of his from college who had also been unlucky in love, but I had no interest in dating anyone. He told me what a great guy he was and how he thought we would be a great match. Yes, of course, I thought sarcastically, I've heard that lie before. He finally gave up.

Work, church and Cliff were occupying my life. In my spare time, I was on a quest for self-discovery. Looking for answers to why my life had been such a train wreck, I turned to the Word of God and self-help books. My search for significance was ever present. I wanted to be the best me that I could be so there would never be a repeat of my former life. Conviction overwhelmed me during every church service, and it felt like every sermon was directed at me. Therefore,

I made a tearful trip to the altar every Sunday. Each time I hoped I would miraculously be healed emotionally. I would feel better temporarily, but soon those destructive emotions would come flooding back. In my search, I discovered that I had to learn to love myself before I could ever expect someone else to love me, and I was clueless about how to even begin to love myself.

Chapter 19

Coincidence or Divine Appointment

There were days when loneliness would engulf me. Friends tried to set me up with guys they knew, but I stayed firm with my conviction to keep romance out of the equation.

One day, I was in downtown Atlanta having lunch with a girlfriend. After lunch, she casually asked me to walk with her over to Peachtree Center to meet a friend of hers. I had a few minutes to kill before I had to be back at work, so I agreed to accompany her. When we arrived, she told the receptionist we were there to see Cary who I assumed was a girl. Little did I realize until I walked into his office that this was yet another attempt for cupid to enter into play. We exchanged polite and cordial conversation, but I was furious. As we left, I told her to mind her own business and not to try to trick me again.

When I got home from work, my friend called and said Cary really liked me and wanted to know if I would go on a double date with her and her boyfriend. I emphatically said, "No, I'm not interested." She was persistent and said if I would go out with him once she would never ask again.

After bantering for quite a while, I reluctantly agreed.

Later that night, the four of us went to dinner. My conversation with Cary came easy, and he appeared to be a real gentleman and quite handsome. We laughed and made small talk. He seemed genuinely interested in getting to know me instead of talking mostly about himself. I confessed to him that I was reluctant to go on the date, but my friend insisted. "Oh my," he said, "She did the same thing to me." We had both been duped.

Realizing their scheme had been discovered, our friends left. Cary and I continued to have an even more interesting conversation. Cary told me he had graduated from Georgia Tech. I said that my partner at work went to Tech also and maybe he knew him. Cary informed me that Georgia Tech was a huge school and the likelihood of knowing my partner was very slim. Out of politeness, he asked his name. When I told him, he gasped. His mouth flew open, and he began laughing hysterically. I asked why he was laughing, and he explained to me that he and my partner were roommates in college at Tech. Cary was the guy that my partner had tried to set me up with. What a coincidence! Or was it?

As our conversation continued, I discovered Cary played in a band called The Night Tides while he was in college. He said his band would play in Daytona Beach during spring break, and I asked if his band ever performed at the Safari Beach Motel. He replied that yes, they did. We both began to laugh out of control as I explained I had also been at that motel during my spring break from high school. In fact, I had a mad crush on Cary as I listened to him sing each night we were there. That event happened ten years before this night. I was living in Tennessee, and he traveled from Atlanta to Daytona Beach, and now ten years later, we were on a date. What a coincidence! Or was it?

We continued to laugh as we realized our connection. It all felt strange but oddly comfortable. Then Cary said, "Hey, let's go see Dan. He'll flip out when we show up together." We drove to my partner's apartment, and when he came to the door and saw us, we all laughed until our stomachs hurt.

What are the odds of two friends on opposite sides of Atlanta unknown to each other attempting to introduce me to the same guy? An amazing coincidence! Or was it?

The night was special, and so was Cary. All the coincidences were thought-provoking. We had a wonderful time, but I could only allow it to be a fun night to remember. Cary called me for another date and said he was being transferred to Florida, to take over leasing and management of a local mall. He said he would really like to see me again before he left. In a way, I was a little sad but relieved that our relationship wouldn't go any further. We agreed to hang out until he moved, and for or the next few weeks, we spent a good deal of time together. We talked a lot about our lives, hopes and dreams. I professed my love for Christ and how important my faith was. Cary said he had never been very religious. He went to church as a child, mostly on holidays, and was never really committed. He couldn't say he had a relationship with Christ but believed he was a good person. He never hurt anyone, and he was happy with his life. I guess he didn't feel a real need for God. I teasingly said I didn't know why he was so happy because he was going to hell. Obviously, I needed to brush up on my witnessing skills.

Chapter 20

Restored by Love

In the blink of an eye, Cary was gone for his new life and career in Florida. I missed him even though I was somewhat relieved that I didn't need to worry about getting too involved. I assumed Cary would go to Florida, meet someone else and forget all about me.

To my surprise, he called a few days later to tell me how much he missed Cliff and me. I had to confess that I missed him too. The following week he drove back to Atlanta to visit us. Something was stirring in us we couldn't deny. Every time we saw each other, our feelings grew. I was terrified. Cary had qualities to which I had not been accustomed in a relationship. He was caring, educated, self-sacrificing and a true gentleman in every way. Oh, did I mention handsome! Cary was the complete package except for the most important missing ingredient. He did not have a committed relationship with Christ.

In time, our visits became more frequent, and each time we parted, I would cry out to God, "Why didn't I meet Cary first? Why did he move so far away and, most importantly, why did I allow myself to fall in love with someone who wasn't completely dedicated to God?" The Lord reminded me of the word I received the night I was about to end my life. If I walked with God, He would give me back what the locusts had eaten. As the conviction of the Lord fell upon me, I knew what I had to do. My life had been derailed by my own foolish decisions, and I made choices for all the wrong reasons. Some were made out of fear, some loneliness and some just plain stupidity. Realizing my folly, I knew I had to make a change. It would be a change that would break my heart, but this time I would do it for God. I promised the Lord the next man in my life would have to make Jesus his number one priority. I was finally making the Lord my partner and leaning on His guidance. As painful as it would be, I had to end my relationship with Cary. Jesus said in Matthew 6:33, "But seek first his kingdom and his righteousness, and all these things will be given to you as well." The Lord had saved me from death and hell, and it was way past time for me to acknowledge Him in my decisions. I was determined not to fail again.

Cary was unaware of my past, so I reasoned that as soon as he heard all the gory details of my past failures, he would hit the door running. After all, why would anyone want to be with such a loser? I still saw myself as used goods, unworthy of love. I had one more trip to Florida to make. The drive was long, and I prayed the whole distance. As the tears streamed down my face, I wondered if God had a plan for my life in spite of my past, but I made a promise I had to keep. Nonetheless, I would trust Him.

Cary was waiting for me and welcomed me with a warm hug and kiss. My heart was beating out of my chest. He prepared dinner and afterward I told him it would be my last trip to visit him. I began to share all the uncomfortable details of my past, he looked at me compassionately. I went on to explain how the long-distance romance was difficult at best and not good for either of us. Besides, I had too much emotional baggage to expect a lasting relationship. And finally, but most importantly, I told him that I had pledged to God that I would only entertain a permanent relationship with someone who was committed to Christ.

As our tears flowed, Cary held me close to him. Then he stepped back, looked into my eyes and said, "It's too late, Dell, I'm in love with you. It doesn't matter about your past or the mistakes you've made. We've all made mistakes." Next, he said, "I believe God brought me into your life to undo all the ugly things that have happened to you. I intend to show you I'm not like those other men. I need you and Cliff in my life, and you need me. You have shown me my need for Christ, and I want to be everything you and Cliff need." Although there was no formal proposal at that moment, we both knew, God willing, we would have a life together.

On my next visit to Florida a few weeks later, Cary and I went to church with our new friends, Gary and Vicki Whitice. At the end of the service, the pastor gave an invitation for salvation. Cary took my hand as we walked to the altar. Cary knelt there and formally received Christ as his Savior. Overcome with joy, I praised God for answering my prayers.

Over the course of the next few months, I began to make preparation for Cliff and me to move to Florida and to start a new life with Cary. There was no doubt that God had orchestrated and blessed our relationship, and on June 4, 1977, we became Mr. and Mrs. Cary Anderson. We were married on Honeymoon Island with a few friends present. It was the happiest day of my life. I was confident Cary, Cliff and I were embarking on a life with Christ as our anchor.

We were truly happy in our new marriage. We grew in the Lord as we pursued Him with all of our hearts. For the first time in my life, I felt loved the way a wife should be loved and cherished. I learned that there is nothing stronger than gentleness.

Several months into our marriage, I found out I was pregnant. We were so excited about adding to our family. However, the demons of my past began to sweep in to steal my joy as the memories of my past began to haunt me. Two marriages had ended in divorce while I was pregnant. After all this time, I still struggled with self-doubt, and I wondered when Cary would walk out the door. With the lingering emotional baggage and fear, I even tried to sabotage our marriage. I began to question and make accusations that Cary was cheating or at least wanted to cheat on me, but even though I was impossible to deal with, Cary continued to reassure me he would never leave. Cary's unfathomable patience was equal to my ever-present insecurity, and the Lord had surely given him an extra measure of grace. As my due date grew closer, I feared God would punish me for having an abortion by taking my baby or giving me a sick baby.

One day at my doctor's office, I had an emotional meltdown and confessed my fears to my Jewish doctor. He took me into his office to console me and reassure me that my baby was fine. He said, "Dell, we may not be of the same faith, but we serve the same God, and the God we serve is not a vindictive God. Stop punishing yourself and enjoy the gift God is giving you." Four months later, I gave birth to a beautiful baby girl with blond hair and blue eyes. We named her Courtney. My God was merciful, and Cary and I were happy beyond belief.

We thought our family was complete, but the Lord had other plans. Five years later, he blessed us with another baby girl with blond hair and blue eyes, and we named her Ashley. What a precious surprise! With her birth, God had indeed restored what the locusts had eaten.

Cary showed me the real meaning of pure agape love. He proved to me that a real man could be gentle, tender and self-sacrificing. He loved deeply and sincerely, and his love wrapped me up like a warm blanket. Our relationship was imperfectly perfect. He lifted me up and comforted me when I was down. When the darts of the enemy were hurled at me, he fought them for me on his knees. He held me when I would awaken from night terrors and reassure me that God was with me, and he even served me communion when I was sick. Plus, Cary was the kind of father that all men should strive to be. The Lord was the center of our lives, and Cary was our spiritual leader. Truly, I was a blessed woman.

As the years passed, God continued to bless our family. We both enjoyed successful careers and prospered as we gained favor in our professions. We enjoyed traveling and the finer things in life. We bought our forever home and enjoyed using it for Christ.

Cary and I became leaders in the church and opportunities began to open up for me to share my testimony of God's amazing grace. I appeared on Christian television and radio broadcasts. It was through ministering to the needs of others that I realized I still needed inner healing myself.

Chapter 21

Choices

It is clear that the choices we make have an impact on all of us as we travel through life with either a positive or negative result. Not only do our choices impact us but also the people that love us. Without God as our partner and the Holy Spirit to guide us, we often make choices we live to regret. Even though we make decisions that grieve God and cause us and others pain, we serve a God who is faithful to forgive. God's Word encourages us, "If we confess our sins, he is faithful and just and will forgive us our sins and purify us from all unrighteousness."
(1 John 1:9)

Forgiveness is a key principle of our Christianity. When we accept Christ as our Savior and ask for forgiveness, He forgives us of all our sins – past and present. He casts our sins into the sea of forgetfulness never to bring them up again. In turn, God says, to be forgiven, we must also forgive those who have sinned against us. "For if you forgive other people when they sin against you, your heavenly Father will also forgive you. But if you do not forgive others their sins, your Father will not forgive your sins." (Matthew 6:14-15) He doesn't say it is a good idea to forgive. No, the Lord commands us to forgive. As I surveyed my past, I realized I had to forgive the atrocities that had been done to me and against me. How could I forgive Jim, who nearly killed me? How could I forgive Bill who caused me to have an abortion?

Then I realized Bill didn't force me to make that terrible decision. I made a choice in desperation, out of fear and a lack of faith that God could and would be with me in my anguish. Sometimes it's easier to blame someone else for our own mistakes instead of taking responsibility for our bad choices. The good news is that in God's Kingdom, failure is never final!

The greater the offense, the harder it was to forgive because I didn't feel forgiveness in my heart. But then the Lord gave me the revelation that forgiveness is not based on our feelings, but on our obedience to our Heavenly Father. So, I chose to forgive as an act of my will. To my surprise, the feelings came when I mouthed the words, "I forgive you." My desire to forgive changed to feelings of true forgiveness. I've heard it said that unforgiveness is like drinking poison and expecting someone else to die. I drank the poison for many years and died a little each day, literally making myself sick.

As a final act to seal the deal, I wrote letters to each of my offenders and confessed how each of their offenses made me feel inside and the struggles I had because of their sins against me. I forgave each person. The letters were never delivered. Instead, I took them to a safe harbor, walked into the water, read each letter aloud, lit a match, burned each one and watched the ashes float out to sea. The process gave me great freedom. I cried tears of release as I put closure to each hurt I had experienced. In so doing, I gave up my desire and need for justice. I thought I had forgiven everyone, but I had overlooked a crucial element in my healing process.

Although it seemed perfect, I realized there was something imperfect in our marriage. I was happy, but there was an aching in my heart, a self-hatred for the decision I made to end my pregnancy years before. Regret and sorrow aren't strong enough words to articulate how I felt. It was a feeling that haunted me every day and prevented me from experiencing the true joy of the Lord. Yes, I was happy with my life and family, but I discovered there is a vast difference between being happy and in being joyful. My self-condemnation had robbed me of experiencing pure joy. You see, it is possible to be happy without joy, and likewise, you can experience the real joy of the Lord in spite of your circumstances.

I made a career of going to the altar begging for forgiveness and peace, but God had already forgiven me. I went to Christian counselors for help. In one session, my counselor asked if I had forgiven myself. Realizing the answer, I repented. You see when the Lord commands us to forgive it includes ourselves. In my mind, this sin was just too horrible to forgive. In so doing, I metaphorically watered down the blood of Jesus. Jesus died once for all our sins. His blood and His grace were more than enough to cover my sin and my guilt. In my mind, I understood, but the concept had not traveled to my heart. The experience of seeing my lifeless baby was too much to forget. I pleaded with God to erase the memory of that awful day. I waited on God, and He listened and heard my prayer. Little did I know the answer was on its way, and it would change my life forever. God had a plan for me that showed His mercy in a way I could only imagine.

Chapter 22

Look Jesus! Mommy's Laughing

Cary and I heard of an evangelist holding a revival in a nearby town. His name was Rodney Howard Brown, and he was a missionary to the United States from South Africa. We heard exciting things about the revival and decided to make the short drive to hear him. As he preached that night, people were filled with the joy of the Lord and holy laughter filled the church.

As the service ended, I was disappointed that I had not been touched as others had. Cary and I left the sanctuary and ran into old friends, Phyllis and Tom Benigas, who had been in the ministry for many years. As we were standing in the lobby chatting, I was overcome with a sense of God's presence. I began to weave back and forth and fell to the floor under the power of God. The service had been dismissed, and hundreds of people were crowded in the lobby. I was told that some people had to step over my body as I lay there glued to the floor. My eyes were closed as the Lord gave me a beautiful vision. It was as if I was watching a movie. I looked up, and to the right, I saw Christ sitting on a large boulder. He was clothed in brilliant white garments, and His face radiated with love and compassion. He held his stomach as He rocked back and forth laughing with sheer joy. The surroundings were gloriously beautiful with brightly colored flowers and colorful trees, and there was a sparkling crystal river that was flowing behind Him that glistened like diamonds from the rays of God's glory. It was the same place that I had seen through the tunnel during my near-death experience after the accident.

The left-hand side of the vision was red and hazy at first, but suddenly the haze began to dissipate. I saw a beautiful little girl with blonde pigtails and big blue eyes laughing and dancing around the feet of Jesus. Then she turned around, swinging her little white dress, stopped dancing and looked down at me. Our eyes met, and I immediately recognized her as my little girl. I reached for her as I sobbed tears of joy. I cried out, "I have to touch her, please let me touch her." My heart was so full of joy that I started to laugh, but oh how I longed to caress her. Phyllis knelt beside me and asked, "What do you see, Dell, what do you see?" Jesus was delighted and was enjoying my little girl as she playfully skipped and danced around His feet, but then I saw and heard something that changed my life forever. She tugged on Jesus' robe and pointed down at me and said, "Look Jesus! Mommy's laughing. Isn't that wonderful?" Jesus replied, "Yes, that's wonderful!" Then Jesus looked at me with such loving eyes and said, "From this day forward, you will no longer minister out of your pain and sorrow, but you will minister out of your joy."

The peace and joy that I felt flooded my entire being. God was so merciful. I had asked Him to remove the memory of my lifeless baby. Instead, because of His great love, He replaced it with a vision of my daughter who clearly loved me and was happy to see that I was joyful.

So many times I had lain in bed at night wondering what she would look like, and now I know she would look just like my two beautiful daughters and me. The supernatural encounter that night made me realize that my fear of her rejection of me in Heaven was unfounded. It will truly be a day of rejoicing when I see Jesus and my daughter face-to-face. The reality of how much the Lord loves me became truth to me that night.

Jesus loves us, oh, how He loves us. He cared about my brokenness and made me whole. His love is more than we can fathom or comprehend. He cares about every aspect of our lives. His love is complete and forever! Nothing we have ever done or ever will do can separate us from His love. His love is unconditional and perfect in every way. His love knows no boundaries, and it gives Him great pleasure when we are happy and in love with Him. He loved us so much that He willingly died to save us from eternal damnation. Knowing how much I love my children, it is inconceivable that He loves us even more. His love is limitless, and there's nothing He won't do to show His love because God is love. We can't earn it, we certainly don't deserve it, but He loves us in spite of our sinful nature. You may think your sin is too great or your pit is too deep, but you are wrong. The enemy has lied to you just as he did to me for such a long time. He is waiting for you to say yes.

Chapter 23

My Dream Fulfilled

As I come to the end of my writing journey, Cary and I have been married for forty-one years. He is truly a gift from God. During our marriage, we have had trials and heartaches as every married couple has experienced. It's called life. But the love and joy we have shared have trumped every trial that we had to overcome. We are not perfect people. We are people who share a perfect love for each other, our family and God.

Although the Lord has touched my life and healed me in many ways, including the night of my near fatal heart attack, I still deal with several health issues. I suffer from PTSD and fibromyalgia as a result of the trauma I have experienced. I have had panic attacks for years that increased during the writing of this book. Reliving the past in such detail has rekindled some painful experiences. When I became aware of these issues, I realized I had to stop writing to deal with them. There were times when the attacks of the enemy were so severe, I wanted to quit, and I questioned if God really wanted me to continue.

On one such evening after a difficult day of writing, I was taxed beyond what I thought I could endure. I sat on the sofa with Cary and shared my heart. I cried out to God in Cary's presence and said I couldn't do it anymore. In my hysteria, I yelled at God and said, "If you don't show me right now that I am supposed to write this book, I will burn my manuscript and never pick up my pen again. I can't do this anymore. I'm not capable. I have no training to write, and it's tearing me apart. I'm serious God; I need you to show me now." I threw my book on the floor and told Cary I was going to bed. I stomped into my room and completed my usual before-bed routine and sat on the side of my bed. I picked up my cell phone to see if I had any messages and turned to Facebook. To my surprise, Rodney Howard Brown was broadcasting live. As I listened, I heard him say, "This lady was so full of guilt and shame, but then God transported her to heaven, and she saw her daughter dancing around the feet of Jesus." At that moment, I knew he was talking about me. My heart was leaping out of my chest as I yelled to Cary to come quickly. "Cary, come here quick, hurry, hurry, he's talking about me." He ran into the room and sat down beside me. We watched and listened as Pastor Rodney continued to minister to his congregation. As they listened, many were being healed and delivered from guilt and shame and began to manifest the joy of their deliverance by running around the sanctuary. They laughed and cried as God was setting them free. Cary and I held each other realizing God had shown up yet again and answered my plea. We were completely in wonder of what an awesome God we serve – He answered me tangibly right then and there! We praised God for His answer until we fell asleep. Cary looked at me and asked, "Who are you that God speaks to you in this way!" I am just a woman who loves God and desires to follow His will for my life. The next day I continued to write, but I had a new fervor to finish the mission to which I had been assigned. It was a wonderful experience for Cary and me to share together.

We have had so many wonderful experiences as we have shared

our lives together. Twenty years ago we were blessed with a grand-son, D.J., who came to live with us when he was six months old because of unforeseen circumstances. He has been such a joy. We adopted him when he was thirteen, and he is pure delight. He has a sister, Selena, living in Tennessee, and we love her too. My daughters, Ashley and Courtney, are a great blessing to us. They are both married to wonderful husbands, and each of them has a son. Those boys, Carson and Lonnie, fill my heart with such love. My daughters have great careers, are happy in their marriages and serve God with all their hearts. Cliff is currently doing well and lives in Tennessee. God has blessed us with a beautiful family that we love dearly.

By the way, my best friend Sandy, who has saved me more times than I can count, typed my manuscript for me. I scribed every word and emailed them to her chapter by chapter. She will always be my best friend and sister from another mother. Phyllis, my friend who knelt beside me when God gave me the vision of my daughter, is now my editor. There is no way I could have finished this assign-ment without the help, prayers and love of my family and friends. I will forever be grateful for their support.

My life has been full. Although I have some health issues, I wait and believe that the Lord will touch me once again. Until then, I know that He is in the waiting! My joy is complete; I have every-thing I could have hoped for and more. My life has been a journey of both heartache and joy, and I realize that I am a trophy of God's grace and love. I give praise to my Lord and Savior for everything through which He has brought me. For forty-one years, He has showered me with great love and favor in every aspect of my life. He has given me the desires of my heart, and I am eternally grate-ful. Even this book has been a gift. I was unsure I could do it, but one day as I was typing I looked up and saw a beautifully framed

151

quote that was given to me by a dear friend, Ruth Lambert, that reads, "The will of God will never take you where the grace of God will not protect you." Surely, "With God, all things are possible." (Matthew 19:26)

Some of you may ask where God was when I was going through all that heartache. My answer is this: The Lord was right there beside me. He was there during every trial and heartbreak and each time I broke His heart. His tears flowed in sync with mine. He waited until I surrendered my will to Him and accepted His will for my life. He has proven His love for me over and over again. I am His princess. I am royalty, and He delights in me. But believe me when I say that He is no respecter of persons. What He has done for me, He will surely do for you. Only Believe!

Chapter 24

An Invitation

As I scribe the final chapter of my book, I wish to speak directly to you. My goal was not just to write an autobiography of my life. The goal was to use my mess as a message to lost and hurting people who may read it. Unless it ministers and brings glory to God, it's just another story.

Perhaps you can relate to one or more of the tragedies I have gone through. Do you need emotional healing from the pain of your past? Do you feel unworthy of love or feel like God overlooks you when you pray? Have you made mistakes that are secret and you can't forgive yourself? Or perhaps others have hurt you so badly that you don't feel you can possibly forgive them. Have you been abused or maybe you've been abandoned? There is no one-size-fits-all when it comes to pain. Have you lost all hope of ever being happy? I felt all of these emotions, and yet I survived through the embrace of the grace of God. You may think you won't make it, but you are stronger than you think. With God as your partner, you can do all things through Christ, His Son.

First of all, do you have a personal relationship with Christ? If not, I John 1:9 reveals how to begin this wonderful relationship with Him, "If we confess our sins, he is faithful and just and will forgive us our sins and purify us from all unrighteousness." If you would like to know the Lord in this way, say the following prayer. If you are sincere when you say it, all your sins will be forgiven, and your sin-stained life will be washed as white as snow. By doing so, you will be assured eternity in Heaven. Let's do it now!

Dear Heavenly Father, I come to you in the name of Jesus. Your Word says in Romans 10:13 that "Everyone who calls on the name of the Lord will be saved." I call upon Your name now, and I confess with my mouth that Jesus is God. I believe in my heart and declare that Jesus Christ is the Son of God and that He was raised from the dead. I repent and turn from my sins, and I accept your forgiveness of all my sins. Jesus, come into my heart and life. I receive You as my personal Lord and Savior. Thank you for saving me now. Amen.

If you prayed this prayer with honesty and sincerity, you are born again, a new creation, and assured of a home in Heaven. "Therefore, if anyone is in Christ, the new creation has come: The old has gone, the new is here!" (2 Corinthians 5:17)

Congratulations! You just made the most important decision of your life. As a follower of Jesus Christ, it doesn't mean you will not have trials and problems, but you will have Christ to guide you and be with you as you take this new path. I promise it will be the most exciting adventure you will ever experience.

I encourage you to reach out to Godly trusted friends. The prayers of my friends were more valuable to me than gold. Get involved in a Bible-based church and read your Bible every day. The Word of God will come alive to you with great meaning and understanding as you seek Him. Talk to God just as you would talk to a friend and then quietly listen. You will sense His presence because you were created to commune with Him. As you offer thanksgiving and praise to Him when you pray, He will inhabit your praise.

Praise the Lord even in your pain and let Him turn your pain to praise. Lay your pain on God's altar and forgive everyone who has hurt you, even if you don't feel like forgiving them. Do it as an act of obedience. Forgive, not because they deserve it, but do it because you deserve it. It's an integral part of your healing. By forgiving others, one more link in the chains that bind you will be broken. If you need professional help, seek Christian counselors. There's no shame in admitting that you need help.

Accept the responsibility for your part in your pain and then forgive yourself. Nothing you have done or will ever do can separate you from God's love and forgiveness. He wants to set you free so that you can live a full life of freedom and joy.

Lastly, don't waste your pain. Use it to help others who are in pain, especially if it mirrors your own pain. Your pain can be someone else's gain. The very pain that brings you the most shame may be the hurt that God will use as your greatest ministry. He wants to use it.

When you've done your part, wait on God. You will find He's in the waiting.

I pray this book will be a catalyst for your healing and deliverance. From my story, I hope you have gleaned the things I did that were helpful and the things that were not, and learn from my mistakes. I pray you, too, will become

Unchained from the pain of your past. May you live in the peace and the freedom of the Lord and walk in His love. Your identity is not defined by your failures or mistakes, but it is defined by who God says that you are and what He decrees over your life. Your Heavenly Father created someone for you to be and planned something for you to do. I pray the following scripture will become your personal testimony as it has been for me:

"I waited patiently for the LORD; he turned to me and heard my cry. He lifted me out of the slimy pit, out of the mud and mire; he set my feet on a rock and gave me a firm place to stand. He put a new song in my mouth, a hymn of praise to our God. Many will see and fear the LORD and put their trust in him." (Psalm 40:1-3)

If you have become unchained through reading this book I would like to hear from you.

Dellanderson.unchained@gmail.com

35438943R00102

Made in the USA
Middletown, DE
06 February 2019